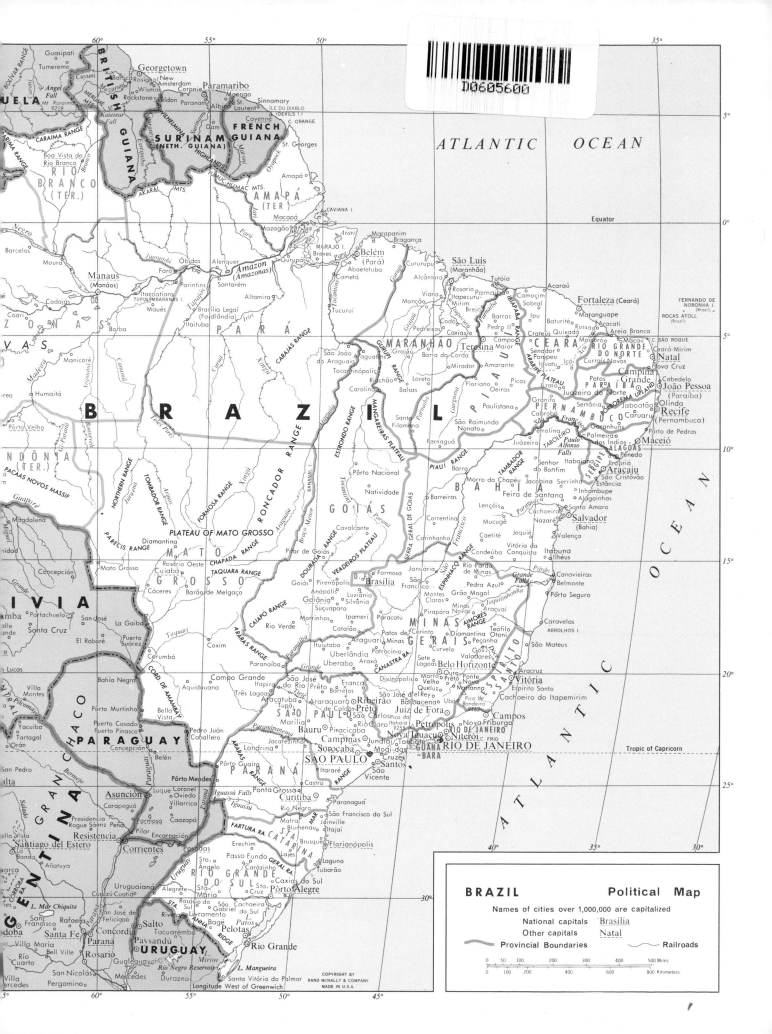

BRAZIL   Political Map

Names of cities over 1,000,000 are capitalized

National capitals   Brasília

Other capitals   Natal

━━━━ Provincial Boundaries   ‿‿‿ Railroads

0   50   100   200   300   400   500 Miles

0   100   200   400   600   800 Kilometers

COPYRIGHT BY
RAND McNALLY & COMPANY
MADE IN U.S.A.

ATLANTIC OCEAN

Equator

Tropic of Capricorn

Longitude West of Greenwich

LIFE WORLD LIBRARY

BRAZIL

OTHER BOOKS BY THE EDITORS OF LIFE

LIFE's Picture History of World War II

LIFE's Picture History of Western Man

The World We Live In
   with Lincoln Barnett

The World's Great Religions

America's Arts and Skills

Picture Cook Book

The Second World War
   with Winston S. Churchill

The Wonders of Life on Earth
   with Lincoln Barnett

LIFE Pictorial Atlas of the World
   with The Editors of Rand McNally

LIFE Nature Library

The Epic of Man

The LIFE Treasury of American Folklore

LIFE WORLD LIBRARY

BRAZIL

by Elizabeth Bishop

and The Editors of LIFE

TIME INCORPORATED   NEW YORK

COVER: Misty clouds drift
across the rounded *morros,*
the hills which keep
Rio de Janeiro huddled close
by the Atlantic Ocean.

ABOUT THE WRITER

Elizabeth Bishop, the author of the interpretive text for this volume of
the LIFE World Library, is an American poet who has made her home in
Brazil since 1952. Widely acquainted in diplomatic, journalistic and artistic circles, she has traveled throughout the country, voyaging to the deso-
late Mato Grosso jungles and far up the Amazon. Born and brought up
in New England, Miss Bishop graduated from Vassar and has been publishing verse and prose for more than 25 years. Her two volumes of
poetry, *North & South* and *A Cold Spring,* in conjunction with work in U.S.
magazines, won her the Pulitzer Prize in 1956.

Contents

		Page
	Introduction	7
Chapter 1	A Warm and Reasonable People	9
Chapter 2	Undeveloped Land of Legend	25
Chapter 3	Century of Honor and Pride	41
Chapter 4	Shifting Centers for Government	53
Chapter 5	The Slow Awakening of a Giant	69
Chapter 6	Graceful and Popular Skills	83
Chapter 7	A Merited Respect for the Arts	97
Chapter 8	A Changing Social Scene	113
Chapter 9	The Struggle for a Stable Democracy	127
Chapter 10	A Nation Perplexed and Uncertain	145
	Appendix	152
	Credits	156
	Index	157

TIME INC. BOOK DIVISION

Editor
NORMAN P. ROSS

Copy Director   *Art Director*
WILLIAM JAY GOLD   EDWARD A. HAMILTON

Chief of Research
BEATRICE T. DOBIE

Editorial staff for "Brazil"

Editor, LIFE World Library	OLIVER E. ALLEN
Assistant to the Editor	JAY BRENNAN
Designer	BEN SCHULTZ
Chief Researcher	GRACE BRYNOLSON
Researchers	REBECCA CHAITIN, IRENE ERTUGRUL, RUTH GALAID, NANCY JONES, HELEN TURVEY, LINDA WOLFE
Picture Researchers	MARGARET K. GOLDSMITH, SUE E. THALBERG
Art Associate	ROBERT L. YOUNG
Art Assistants	JAMES D. SMITH, RICHARD FORTE
Copy Staff	MARIAN GORDON GOLDMAN, ANN SHAW, CAROL HENDERSON, DOLORES LITTLES

•

Publisher	JEROME S. HARDY
General Manager	JOHN A. WATTERS

•

LIFE MAGAZINE

Editor   *Managing Editor*   *Publisher*
EDWARD K. THOMPSON   GEORGE P. HUNT   C. D. JACKSON

•

The text for the chapters of this book was written by Elizabeth Bishop, and the picture essays were written by Walter Karp. The following members of the LIFE Magazine staff helped in producing the book: Dmitri Kessel, Leonard McCombe and Frank J. Scherschel, staff photographers; Hugh Moffett, Assistant Managing Editor; and Doris O'Neil, Chief of the LIFE Picture Library.

Valuable assistance was also provided by the following staff members of Time Inc.: Donald Bermingham and Eileen MacKenzie of the Foreign News Service; John Blashill and Jayme Dantas of the Rio de Janeiro Bureau; George de Carvalho, former Bureau Chief in Rio de Janeiro; Content Peckham, Chief of the Bureau of Editorial Reference; and Berta Gold of TIME Magazine.

Introduction

Traditional friend of the United States, Brazil is a fascinating and exotic country. Its new capital, Brasília, rises austerely on the endless rolling central plateau. The majestic Amazon flows through the tropical jungles of the north. Bahia is a city of lovely old churches and colorful street life. Rio de Janeiro, on the coast, is endowed with a natural beauty unsurpassed by any other city in the world. São Paulo, to the south, is the greatest industrial center in Latin America, proud product of Paulista dynamism.

Despite the advances made in the energetic cities, Brazil's sterile plains, its great solitudes, its enormous swamps and desertlike wastelands make the country a land of the frontier. Brazil has incalculable mineral resources and lands rich in coffee, cocoa, cotton and a variety of other agricultural products. Their plenitude contrasts with the poverty of the squalid *favelas* of Rio and other cities, and with the misery of northeastern Brazil. Life varies from the sophistication of the great capitals to the primitive ways of savage Indians.

So much and more the casual visitor to Brazil may see. But Brazil is not a mere geographical expression, or a mass of bricks and stones; it is a nation of the spirit. Brazilians are proud of the fact that different races have learned to live together in harmony in their country. They are proud, too, of a culture which has made a world mark in architecture, literature, painting and music. And they are proud of Brazil's great contributions to inter-American ideals. They have a warmth of hospitality that matches the warmth of the tropical sun.

There is a growing sense of democracy in Brazil, as well as a sense of vigor and destiny and of confidence in Brazil's future. Brazil aspires to realize its potential grandeur.

All of these things and more are treated in this book published by the Editors of LIFE. The magnificent picture essays supplement Miss Bishop's brilliant text in order to bring the reader a better understanding of our South American sister republic. It is a timely volume. For misunderstanding is the handmaiden of ignorance; and friendship, understanding and cooperation between Brazil and the United States were never more necessary than they are today.

JOHN MOORS CABOT
former U.S. Ambassador to Brazil

Under a blazing sun, visitors to Brasília stroll on a rooftop promenade in the new inland capital. A large number of them trek

A Warm and Reasonable People

1

many miles from the surrounding scrubland areas to admire the magnificent city the federal government has planted in their midst.

RECENTLY in Rio de Janeiro one of those "human interest" dramas took place, the same small drama that takes place every so often in New York or London or Rome: a newborn baby was kidnaped from a maternity hospital. Her name was Maria da Conceição, or Mary of the Conception, but the newspapers immediately abbreviated this, Brazilian-fashion, to Conceiçãozinha, or "Little Conception."

Conceiçãozinha made the headlines for a week, and while she did it is safe to say that the country's current inflation, the soaring cost of living, the shifts of power in the government—perhaps even the soccer scores—took second place for most readers.

The hospital staff was questioned. A feeble-minded woman wandering in the neighborhood was detained. The police poked into culverts and clumps of weeds and around the *favelas*, Rio's notorious hillside slums. Somehow the kidnaping was kept from the baby's mother, but the young government-worker father was photographed at his desk, in postures of despair. Then, after three days, Conceiçãozinha was found, safe and sound. One of the hospital nurses, who had lost a child of her own by miscarriage shortly before, had stolen her.

SO far it all could have happened in New York, London or Rome. But now the story becomes Brazilian. The white nurse's mulatto lover, owner of a small grocery store, had promised her a house to live in if she had a child, and he had already given her the equivalent of 50 dollars for the baby's layette. So the nurse—determined, she told reporters, "to have a decent place to live in" with "home atmosphere," and also because she really wanted a baby—concealed her miscarriage and told her lover that the baby would be born on such and such a day. Until then she boarded Conceiçãozinha with her laundress, an old woman living in a *favela* shack. The nurse was arrested as she took them food. The baby was fat and well. The laundress, who could not read, knew nothing of the hubbub in the papers and protested her complete innocence. When the father was told the good news he sobbed and said, "This is the strongest emotion I have ever felt in my life." He was photographed embracing the police. Conceiçãozinha was taken back to the hospital, where "the doctors were shouting and the nurses weeping." Three or four hundred people had gathered outside. The swaddled baby was held up to a window, but the crowd screamed, "Show her little face!" So it was shown "to applause and cheers."

The next day the drama continued on a lower plane but in even more Brazilian style. The two sets of in-laws quarreled as to which one would have the honor of harboring the child and her real mother first. One grandmother denied that the chief of police had been asked to be Conceiçãozinha's godfather, because "that is always a *family* affair." And the poor father was faced with fulfilling his *promessas*. If the baby was found alive, he had promised (1) to pay for four Masses; (2) to stop smoking for a year;

(3) to give two yard-high wax candles, as well as a life-size wax model of a baby, to the Church of Our Lady of the Penha; and (4) to climb the steps of the same church on his knees, carrying a lighted candle. This 18th Century church perches on top of a weirdly shaped *penha*, or rock, that sticks up out of the plain just north of the city. It is a favorite church for pilgrimages and for the fulfilling of *promessas*. The steps up to it number 365.

THE story of Conceiçãozinha contains a surprising amount of information about Brazilian life, manners and character. Much of it, of course, is what one might expect to find in any Latin American country. Brazilians love children. They are highly emotional and not ashamed of it. Family feeling is very strong. They are Roman Catholics, at least in outward behavior. They are franker than Anglo-Saxons about extramarital love, and they are tolerant of miscegenation. Also—as one would expect in a very poor and in many ways backward country—many people are illiterate; there are feeble-minded people at large who in other countries might be in institutions; and hospitals may not always be run with streamlined efficiency. So far it is all fairly predictable.

But there is more to it than that. The story immediately brings to mind one of Brazil's worst, and certainly most shocking, problems: that of infant mortality. Why all this sentimental, almost hysterical, concern over one small baby, when the infant mortality rate in Brazil is still one of the highest in the world? The details of Conceiçãozinha's story are worth examining not only for the interesting light they throw on that contradictory thing, the Brazilian character, but also because the tragic, unresolved problem they present is almost a paradigm of a good many other Brazilian problems, big and small.

First there is the obvious devotion to children. As in other Latin countries, babies are everywhere. Everyone seems to know how to talk to infants or dandle them, and unselfconsciously. It is said that two kinds of small business never fail in Brazil, infants' wear shops and toy shops. The poorest workman will spend a disproportionate amount of his salary for a christening dress (or for milk if he happens to know it is vital to his child's health). Parents love to dress up their offspring; the children's costume balls are an important part of Carnival every year throughout the country.

In Catholic Brazil there is no divorce and no legalized birth control, and large families are the rule. Sometimes families run to 20 or more, and five or six children is the average. Brazil is a very young country; more than 52 per cent of the population is under 19 years old. Early marriage is normal, and a baby within a year is taken for granted. Children are almost always wanted—the first three or four of them, at least—and adored.

And yet the infant mortality rate stays appallingly high. In the poorest and most backward regions of the great northeast bulge and the Amazon basin, it is as high as 50 per cent during the first year of life, sometimes even higher. The cities of Recife and Rio, with their large *favelas,* are two of the worst offenders. During the three days when Conceiçãozinha was hidden in the washerwoman's shack, and survived, it is a safe guess that more than 60 babies died in Rio.

MOST of this tragic waste of life is due to malnutrition, which weakens a person's resistance to disease. But often the malnutrition is due not so much to actual lack of food as to ignorance, a vicious circle in which poverty creates ignorance which then creates more poverty. In Rio, for example, there are many good free clinics. But fine doctors have been known to resign after working in them for years; they can no longer endure seeing the same children brought in time after time, sicker, weaker and finally dying because the parents are too ignorant, or too superstitious, to follow a few simple instructions.

The masses of poor people in the big cities, and the poor and not-so-poor of the "backlands," love their children and kill them with kindness by the thousands. The wrong foods, spoiled foods, worm medicines, sleeping syrups —all exact a terrible toll: the "little angels" in paper-covered, gilt-trimmed coffins, blue for boys and pink for girls.

Nevertheless, the population of Brazil is increasing rapidly. Life expectancy has gone up considerably in the last few decades. The indomitable and apparently increasing vitality of Brazil shines through the grimmest death toll statistics. It is like the banana tree that grows everywhere in the country. Cut it back to a stump above ground, and in a matter of days it sends up a new shoot and starts unfolding new green leaves.

INDEED, the banana tree is a fairly good symbol for the country itself and for what has happened and is still happening to it. Brazil struck all the early explorers as a "natural paradise," a "garden," and at its best moments it still gives that impression—a garden neglected, abused and still mostly uncultivated, but growing vigorously nevertheless. Great resources have been squandered, but even greater ones are still there, waiting. Barring some worldwide disaster, material prosperity seems bound to arrive. But it is the mismanagement and waste of both human and material wealth along the way that shocks the foreigner as well as the educated, sensitive Brazilian. To give only one example of this: because of inadequate roads, poor transportation and a widespread lack of refrigeration, some 40 per cent of all food produced spoils before it reaches the big markets.

Exploding birth rate and infant mortality, great wealth and degrading poverty—these are the two big paradoxes. But along with them come many smaller ones repeating the pattern, overlapping and interacting: passionate and touching patriotism combined with constant self-criticism and denigration; luxury and idleness (or admiration of them) combined with bursts of energy; extravagance and pride, with sobriety and humility. The same contrasts even appear in Brazilian history, periods of waste and corruption alternating with periods of reform and housecleaning.

Brazil is very big and very diverse. Brazilians vary widely from one region to another. A man may be a "Carioca" (from Rio—the name probably comes from an Indian expression meaning "white man's home"), a "Paulista" (from São Paulo), a "Mineiro" (from the state of Minas Gerais) or a "Bahiano" (from the state of Bahia), and he is proud of the peculiarities of his own region.

But not only does he vary geographically, he varies historically. Men from two, three or more eras of European history live simultaneously in Brazil today. The coastal cities, from Belém at the mouth of the Amazon River to Pôrto Alegre in the south, are filled with 20th Century men with 20th Century problems on their minds: getting on in the world and rising in it socially; how to pay for schools and doctors and clothes. Then in the surrounding countryside is a rural or semirural population who lead lives at least half a century behind the times, old-fashioned both agriculturally and socially. And for the people of the fishing villages, for those living on the banks of the great rivers, for cowboys and miners—all the backlands people—time seems to have stopped in the 17th Century. Then, if one ventures even a little farther on, one enters the really timeless, prehistoric world of the Indians.

AND yet there is one factor that unites Brazil more closely than some European countries which are only as big as a single Brazilian state: its language. Brazil is the largest Portuguese-speaking country in the world. Its Portuguese differs from that spoken in Portugal at least as much as American English differs from English English. But throughout Brazil the language is amazingly uniform, and Brazilians have no difficulty understanding each other.

It is a rather heavy and solemn tongue, with some of its grammatical forms actually dating back to the Latin of the Roman Republic. The tendency in Brazil is to be careless about grammatical niceties, at least in speaking, and to lighten the language with constant diminutives (as Maria da Conceição became Conceiçãozinha). In fact the Portuguese regard Brazilian Portuguese as "effeminate"—charming when women speak it, but no language for men.

Not only the constant use of diminutives, but also the forms of address help create an atmosphere of familiarity, of affection and intimacy. Brazilian nomenclature is almost as complicated as Russian and is often compared to it, but in general women are addressed by "Dona" followed by the Christian name or pet name, and men by "Doutor" if they have a university degree or a sufficient degree of prosperity, or, if they have not, by a softened form of Senhor, "Seu," again followed by the Christian name.

BRAZILIANS are very quick, both emotionally and physically. Like the heroes of Homer, men can show their emotions without disgrace. Their superb *futebol* (soccer football) players hug and kiss each other when they score goals, and weep dramatically when they fail to. Brazilians are also quick to show sympathy. One of the first and most useful words a foreigner picks up is *coitado* (poor thing!).

Part of the same emotionalism in social life is the custom of the *abraço*, or embrace. Brazilians shake hands a great deal, and men simultaneously embrace each other casually with their free arms. Women often embrace, too, and kiss rapidly on both cheeks: *left! right!* Under strong feeling the *abraço* becomes a real embrace.

A rich man will shake hands with and embrace a poor man and also give him money, try to find him a job and pay his wife's doctor bills, because they grew up on the same *fazenda,* or country estate, made their first communions together and perhaps are even "brothers of creation," a system of partial adoption that dates from slavery days. Servants are still often called *criados*, a term which originally meant they had been raised in the family. Even today one occasionally sees an elegant lady out walking, leaning on the arm of a little dressed-up

Negro girl, or taking tea or orangeade with her in a tearoom; the little girl is her "daughter of creation" whom she is bringing up.

In such relationships there is complete ease of manner on both sides. Sometimes Brazilians seem to confuse familiarity with democracy, although the attitude seems rather to be a holdover from slavery days, or feudalism, or even from the Roman Empire, when every rich man had his set of poor relations and parasites. Nevertheless, a sense of natural responsibility underlies the relationship and certainly contributes something toward the more difficult and somewhat broader conception of what democracy generally means today.

Home and family are very important in Brazil. But because there is no divorce, strange situations arise: second and third "marriages," unrecognized legally but socially accepted, in which there are oddly mixed sets of children. These situations merely give the Brazilians a chance to exercise their unique talent for kindly tolerance. In fact, in the spirit of mollification the courts more than two decades ago ruled that henceforth no one could be legally termed illegitimate.

There is a story about Rio de Janeiro and its beloved, decrepit *bondes* or open trolley cars. A *bonde* was careening along, overcrowded as usual, with men hanging to the sides like a swarm of bees. It barely stopped for a tall, gangling man to get off; and as he jumped from the step he fell, landing in a humiliating heap. His fellow passengers laughed. He pulled himself together, got up and with great dignity shouted after them: "Everyone descends from the *bonde* in the way he wants to."

That is the perfect statement of the Brazilian belief in tolerance and forebearance: everyone should be allowed to descend from the *bonde* in his or her own way.

The greatest tolerance is naturally extended to love, because in Brazil that is always the most important emotion. Love is the constant element in almost every news story, street scene or familiar conversation. If lunch is an hour or so late because the cook has been dawdling with the pretty delivery boy, her mistress will

PORTUGUESE AND SPANISH: THEIR SIMILARITIES AND DIFFERENCES

Portuguese, the language of Portugal and Brazil, is not only an old neighbor of Spanish in both the Iberian peninsula and South America, but a close kin as well. Like French, Italian and Romanian, the two languages have evolved from dialects of Latin. Neither one is an offshoot of the other. Like brothers, they have a common parentage, but they have gone their separate ways for so long that a speaker of Spanish would not understand Portuguese if he were hearing it for the first time. Phonetically the two languages differ sharply. Portuguese (like French) nasalizes vowels that precede the consonants "m" or "n." This is unknown in Spanish. In many such words the consonant drops out completely and a tilde sign (˜) over the nasalized vowel is all that remains of the "m" or "n" sound. The vocabularies are similar, but a good number of Spanish words are utterly unlike the equivalent Portuguese words. Between the Portuguese spoken in Portugal and the Portuguese spoken in Brazil the differences are mostly in intonation. But the Brazilian version has 10,000 more words than the mother tongue, most of them introduced by Indians and Negroes.

	Spanish	Portuguese		Spanish	Portuguese
window	ventana	janela	health	salud	saúde
street	calle	rua	the	el or la	o or a
hat	sombrero	chapéu	leg	pierna	perna
knife	cuchillo	faca	door	puerta	porta
bread	pan	pão	man	hombre	homen
wool	lana	lã	game	juego	jôgo
are	son	são	woman	mujer	mulher
sky	cielo	céu	church	iglesia	igreja

scold her, even lose her temper (for Brazilian tempers are quick, too), but there will be sympathy underneath and the cook's excuse will be frank, half humorous, possibly even indecent from the Anglo-Saxon point of view. "First things first" is the motto. Opposed to the constant preoccupation with love is the lack of sentimentality about marriage arrangements. There may be surface emotionalism, but there is Latin logic and matter-of-factness underneath.

A Brazilian woman shopping in New York was puzzled by the tag on a madras shirt she had bought for her husband: "Guaranteed to fade." In a country as rich as the United States, why would anyone want to wear faded clothes? Why do the Americans like to wear faded blue jeans? Surely that is false romanticism and just one more example of the childishness of the Anglo-Saxon as compared to the more adult Latin? Values are simple and realistic in Brazil. Outside of fashionable circles, the poor are thin and the rich are fat, and fat is a sign of beauty, as it has been since the ancients.

Brazilians are in many ways quick, but they can also be woefully slow. The same mistress who scolds her cook for flirting will complain about the meals always being late. Yet if anyone asks naively, "But why not have lunch at one o'clock every day?" she will reply, "Oh, well—this isn't a factory."

AMONG the first settlers in Brazil were the big "captains," impoverished Portuguese noblemen and younger sons seeking quick fortunes, who were used to having feudal henchmen and slaves around them. They and the Portuguese of low rank who were also early on the scene soon established a tradition of having Indian and Negro slaves. One result is that to this day physical labor is looked down upon. Of all his inherited attitudes this one is the hardest for the Brazilian, free of so many other prejudices, to overcome. The upper-class Brazilian who visits the bustling North American continent cannot understand why there is so much eagerness for work. A rich boy mowing the lawn? More romanticism! A

lifetime government job, white-collar work, or preferably no work at all, is the poor man's dream. A shabby, sickly bill collector, who can barely support his wife and six children, but who proudly carries a brief case and wears two fountain pens in his pocket, will tremble with rage if his position in society is misunderstood: "I?—Everyone knows I have never worked with my hands in my life!"

BUT along with admiration for a life of ease and luxury goes a strange indifference to physical comfort. Even in cold weather—and it can get quite cold south of São Paulo or in the higher regions of the interior—there is no heating of any kind. People simply put on more clothes. In the small towns in June or July, the coldest months, one often sees a pleasant, old-fashioned Brazilian scene: the large family, grandparents, parents, babies, visiting godparents, and a few odd cousins and fiancés, wearing sweaters or perhaps bathrobes over their clothes, all sitting around the dining-room table under a hanging lamp. Everyone is doing exactly what he wants: reading the paper, playing cards or chess, or relentlessly arguing over the other people's heads. Elsewhere, even the *granfinos*, the elegant, cosmopolitan-rich set of the upper class, who have adopted the "English weekend" and spend it in Petrópolis or other resorts, present somewhat the same air of camping out in the winter. In freezing rooms, the ladies with mink coats over their slacks and rugs over their knees, the gentlemen wearing mufflers, they watch after-dinner movies, the latest chic diversion. Perhaps they will sip Scotch, again to be chic, but more likely *cafézinhos*, the boiling hot and very sweet little cups of coffee. The poor, meanwhile, drink the same *cafézinhos*, pile all their clothes on top of them and go to bed early.

Brazilians are a remarkably sober people. Two or three *cafézinhos* provide enough fuel for them to talk and argue on all night long. The late 19th Century sailor-author Captain Joshua Slocum (*Sailing Alone Around the World*) was, in his earlier days, in command of a ship on the South American coast. He speaks more than once of "my sober Brazilian sailors" who, unlike the sailors of other nationalities, always turned up again after a night in port with no hang-overs.

Perhaps because Brazilians are usually as indifferent to cooking as they are to physical comfort, the food is very bad. The staple diet is rice, dried meat and black beans, cooked with a great deal of lard and garlic and served with a dish of manioc flour, to be sprinkled over the beans. However, there are many dishes of great refinement that use 20 or 30 ingredients, and wonderful desserts with even more wonderful names like Maiden's Drool, Bride's Pillow and Blessed Mothers (small cakes).

THE conversation in the caffeine-enlivened evenings will alternate between politics, real estate deals (a favorite pastime of all classes) and family reminiscences. Proud of their Latin logic, Brazilians are also a little proud of their reputation for "craziness." Family traits are cherished; such and such a family will be famous for its bad temper or for its obstinacy or for its green eyes—because looks, too, are very important. A good family nose will be traced down right to the last-born infant. This preoccupation with good looks may come from the knowledge that many of the oldest families have some Negro blood. There is a popular notion that famous beauties should have a drop or two of such blood in their veins; it is supposed to make them more vivacious. Since everyone also wants to be as *claro*, or white, as possible, this is another of those contradictions that seem to bother no one.

Criticizing the country, running down the government and talking about the "national stupidity" with fearful and apocryphal examples are also favorite pastimes. It is sometimes hard to tell whether the speakers are really angry or merely excited, tolerant or unaware of any need for tolerance, naive or extremely sophisticated. Brazilians are mercurial: recently during Carnival a Negro dancing along the sidewalk with his wife suddenly ran into his two

mistresses. There was a small riot and some hair-pulling, but an hour later all four were observed gaily dancing the samba together and holding hands. When the wife was asked why she put up with it, she answered helplessly but rather proudly, "He talked me into it. He's such a pretty talker!"

More taciturn peoples are likely to be suspicious of talkative ones and to think they are wasting their energy. One frequently meets among intellectuals a sort of Brazilian Hamlet-type, incapable of serious work or action, who seems to be covering up a deep anxiety with words, words, words, a pretended madness, a deliberately fanciful humor that is not frivolity although it resembles it. The earthy humor of the poor, the brutal cartoons in newspapers and magazines, the street boys who laugh at cripples or ugly women—this is directly in line with the humor of the Romans; but the humor of the intellectual is very different, wry, gentle and a little wild.

They poke fun at their usually bloodless revolutions: "No one fought in that revolution—it was the rainy season." Like the Portuguese form of bullfighting in which there is no killing, Brazilian revolutions or *golpes* (coups) sometimes seem to be little more than political and rhetorical maneuvering. A man's speeches, his moral and physical courage, are admired, but actual violence is going too far. Duels are still fought in Argentina, but they are out of style in Brazil. Brazil has not fought a major war for almost a century. It has rarely wanted more land, already having more than it knows what to do with.

JOKES tell even more. There is an old favorite, perhaps not even Brazilian originally, about a man walking down the street with a friend. He is grossly insulted by a stranger, and says nothing. The friend tries to rouse his fighting instincts, "Didn't you hear what he called you? Are you going to take that? Are you a man, or aren't you?" The man replies, "Yes, I'm a man. But not *fanatically*." This is the true Brazilian temper.

The Magnetic Force Exerted by Cities

Although more than half the Brazilian population lives off the land, Brazil is mainly a city civilization. The urban centers soak up the nation's resources, house its best talents and dominate its politics. Migration to the cities is fast emptying the already half-empty rural areas. It is said that even the pioneers in Mato Grosso want only to become rich enough to retire to São Paulo. For more and more Brazilians, the good life means life in the big city.

COMMUTER CROWDS festoon an open trolley car that takes them to a busy square in downtown Rio de Janeiro. When Rio's vintage trolley cars become filled up, agile passengers simply jump on board and hang on tight.

VIVID CONTRAST is preserved in Rio where a tidy 18th Century Catholic church stands before the sleek Ministry of Education and Health, a building which attracted international attention when it was begun in the 1930s.

*URBAN STYLE of life
has all the modern
trimmings of elegant
display, high fashion
and bustling commerce*

DEMURE BEAUTY, a Rio film actress (*opposite*) sits by a giant tropical tree raised in the city's Botanical Garden.

YOUNG SPORTSMEN drop in at the Rio Jockey Club (*right*), a favorite haunt of the Brazilian upper class.

SHOPPING STREET in São Paulo (*below*) is lined with parked cars. The city is the center of Brazilian auto making.

RIVER CRAFT moor at Belém as an oncoming squall darkens the sky. Gateway to the Amazon Valley, Belém waxed rich when the area held a world rubber monopoly.

COLONIAL HOUSES lining a hillside street in Bahia were built in the days when the sugar-exporting city was a thriving center of wealth, learning and political power.

CREAMY ARC of Rio de Janeiro's world-famous Copacabana Beach hooks seaward from a spur of the coastal hills. Though it is no longer the nation's capital, Rio remains the leading city. A social center for the elite, it is also a magnet for the poor, who leave the countryside in droves to live on the hilltops overlooking the Rio harbor.

2

Undeveloped Land of Legend

IN one of the parks of Rio stands a fine, flamboyant example of Latin American park sculpture, a much-bigger-than-life-size man dressed in a costume-pageant outfit with wide fur-trimmed sleeves and a skirt, holding onto a ton or so of undulated bronze banner. One side of the pedestal says "1900" and the other, "1500." The statue was set up to commemorate what authorities believe to be the 400th anniversary of the discovery of Brazil by the Portuguese navigator Pedro Alvares Cabral. As the city has grown, this statue has been shunted about, and in somewhat the same way historians have shuffled the problem of whether Cabral should be called the discoverer of Brazil or not. But they all agree that he at least was the first to claim it—in 1500, shortly after Easter.

But a land called "Brasil" was a legend in Europe at least as early as the Ninth Century. Wherever it was, it was the place where *bresilium* came from, a wood obtained in trade with the Far East and much in demand for dyeing cloth red. Columbus found the dyewood tree in the West Indies, but in his eagerness for gold he simply ignored it. But the first European ships that were sent back from the continent of South America were loaded with brazilwood, and "Brazil," or "Brasil," became the common name for the new country.

Pedro Alvares Cabral was supposedly on his way directly to India in command of a fleet of 13 ships; if so, he was off his course by several hundred miles. Since the best astronomers, mathematicians and professors of navigation of the day were employed at the court of King Manuel I of Portugal, it scarcely seems possible that Cabral's side trip was accidental. Probably the powerful Portuguese were really trying to get ahead of the Spaniards, who were exploring the lands farther north.

In theory, there should have been no rivalry between the two powers. Two years after Columbus's first voyage in 1492, Portugal and Spain, then at the height of their age of discoveries, had grandly divided all the non-Christian world between them. The Treaty of Tordesillas, sanctioned by the Pope, gave Portugal all the lands east of a line drawn 370 leagues west of the Cape Verde Islands; all the lands west of the line were to go to Spain. The exact position of this line was always vague, and the rivalry between the two countries was so strong that even after the treaty they tried to conceal their discoveries from each other. But Portugal believed, or pretended to believe, that all of Brazil was within its rightful territories. The result was that almost half of South America became a Portuguese colony, while most of the rest was colonized by Spain.

ON Cabral's flagship there was a nobleman-merchant named Pero Vaz de Caminha, who had signed on as scribe. The wonderfully vivid letter he wrote to King Manuel, describing Brazil and the Tupi Indians, the first of the many tribes the Portuguese were to encounter, has been called "the first page in the history of Brazil" and, with equal justice, "the first page of Brazilian literature." After a brief account of the voyage Caminha calmly announces:

"On this day at the vesper hours we caught sight of land, that is, first of a large mountain, very high and round, and of other lower lands to the south of it, and of flat land, with great groves of trees. To this high mountain the captain gave the name of *Monte Pascoal* [Easter Mountain], and to the land, *Terra da Vera Cruz* [Land of the True Cross]."

The mountain, in the present state of Bahia, still bears the same name. The king, however, changed Vera Cruz to Santa Cruz (Holy Cross), which remained the official name until the middle of the century, when, over ecclesiastical protests, it became Brazil. But on the first maps it is either "Brazil" or the "Land of Parrots." Along with dyewood, macaws had been sent back to Europe, and their brilliant colors, large size and loud shrieks obviously had made a deep impression. On a world map published in Europe the year after Cabral's return (*opposite*), the coastline of Brazil is not much more than a guess, but Caminha's groves of trees are there, lined up as formally as in a Portuguese garden, and under them sits a group of giant macaws, presumably to give explorers some idea of what to expect.

EVEN if the name Vera Cruz was not very original in the 16th Century, it was an obvious choice for Cabral. He was a Knight of the Order of Christ, and the fleet's sails and banners bore the Order's red cross. The men landed to celebrate Easter Sunday with Mass, and set up a cross. And for many nights at sea they had all been watching the brilliant stars of the Southern Cross overhead; the fleet astronomer wrote to the king to describe this useful constellation. Ever since, Brazil has felt itself to be uniquely "The Land of the Southern Cross." The highest decoration awarded to foreigners is the Order of the Southern Cross; the present unit of money, the cruzeiro, is named for it—and so are thousands of bars, restaurants, business firms and manufactured products. And in keeping with the frequent Brazilian abruptness of transition between the material and the spiritual, the 1,000-cruzeiro note bears a portrait of Cabral on one side and an engraving of that first Easter Mass on the other.

Caminha was a good reporter. He describes the Indians' looks and behavior, their food and houses, the strange new wildlife. The Indians

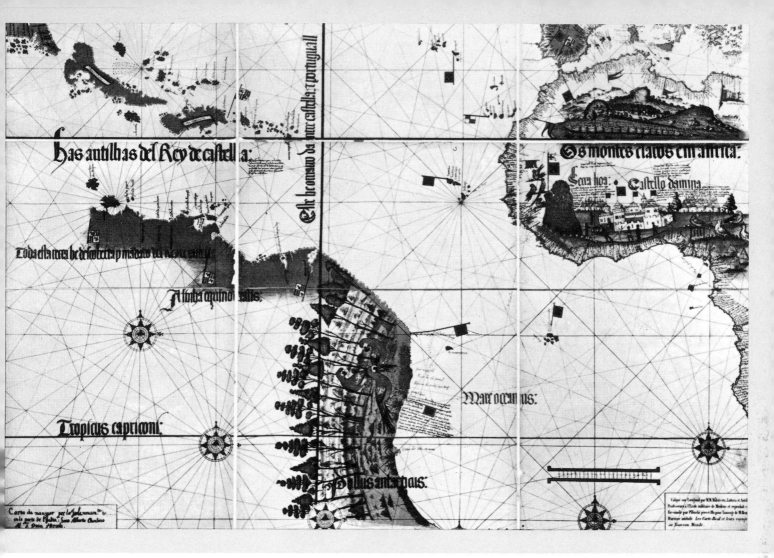

Has antilhas del Rey de castella.

Os montes claros em affica.

Toda ella costa he descoberta p madado del Rey enrriq̄.

A linha equinoccial.

Tropicus capricorni.

Mare oceanus.

Ilhas antarticas.

A STRANGE NEW WORLD for Europeans, Brazil appears on this section of a 1502 world map as a tree-fringed area containing macaws. Brazil's jagged coastline is mostly guesswork. By contrast, the African coast is fairly accurate and even the islands of the Antilles are shown in their approximate positions. The longitudinal marker slicing Brazil is the famed Treaty of Tordesillas line. As the map indicates, the *Rey de Castella* (meaning the King of Spain) owns all the lands west of it. The Portuguese were granted all the land to the east. This amicable arrangement was upset by Portuguese colonists, who pushed west of the line to claim the rest of what is now Brazil.

were friendly and docile—too docile for their own good. Presents were exchanged, one of which was grimly prophetic: the Indians gave the Portuguese headdresses of their exquisite featherwork, and in return the Portuguese gave them the red caps worn by laborers. The Indians attended the Mass and mimicked the white men, kneeling, crossing themselves and singing a hymn of their own.

The Portuguese mercifully lacked the blood-thirsty missionary zeal of the Spaniards. But Caminha, perhaps because he felt it was expected of him, wrote: "Our Lord gave them fine bodies and good faces as to good men;

and He who brought us here, I believe, did not do so without purpose." The Indians were "so clean, so fat and so beautiful" that they appeared to be healthier and stronger than the Portuguese themselves. As for the women, Caminha noted of one that "she was so well built and so rounded and her lack of shame was so charming, that many women of our land seeing such attractions, would be ashamed that theirs were not like hers." The Portuguese had always been romantically drawn to women of darker races; they had long taken Moorish wives and Negro concubines, and there were already many Negro slaves in Portugal. In Brazil it was only

27

natural for them to become eager miscegenationists almost immediately.

Caminha reported that they had seen neither gold, nor silver, nor any other metal. But he added that the interior appeared to be very large: "Its waters are quite endless. So pleasing is it that if one cares to cultivate it, everything will grow. . . ." The phrase, *Em se plantando, dá* (If you plant it, it will bear) is now a familiar saying, but it has changed its meaning. Once a promise, it is now used in ironic reproach to anyone who neglects obvious opportunities. That simple reversal of meaning reveals a great deal about the long history of the undeveloped resources and possibilities of Brazil since the year 1500.

ON his departure, Cabral left behind two convicts, who were last seen bewailing their fate while the Indians tried to console them. The condemned men were under orders to learn the Indians' language and to convert them to the true faith. This was the usual Portuguese practice; no one knows how many hundreds of these wretched men were dropped along the coast by later expeditions. Most vanished forever, but here and there one survived and became a "great chief," took many Indian wives and produced many children. The *caboclo* (half Indian and half Portuguese) daughters of the early adventurers were ready to marry the next generation of Portuguese that arrived, and in this way a solid foundation was laid for a mixed, and easily mixable, race.

Early Brazilian history abounds in fascinating personalities: condemned convicts, devout Jesuit missionaries (St. Ignatius Loyola's order was founded in 1540) and Portuguese noblemen, often younger sons, who became the "great captains" appointed by the crown and given almost kingly powers. But this oddly assorted crew had found no gold; there were no cities to ransack, and for the first quarter of the century Brazil was left almost untouched. Indeed, the settlers had no way of knowing how vast the new land was—or how promising it would prove to be in later centuries.

Everyone today seems to know at least two facts about this half-a-continent that became Brazil: it is bigger than the United States was before Alaska became a state, and the seasons there are the reverse of those in the northern hemisphere. It is big, stretching from north of the equator to south of the Tropic of Capricorn, and west to the foothills of the Andes— an area of 3.3 million square miles. But to say that the seasons are reversed is too simple; all the accidents of geography combine to change the pattern. Caminha thought the climate "temperate," and although his conclusion was based on the scantiest evidence, it turned out to be more or less right.

Brazil is tropical and subtropical, with few extremes of temperature. The Amazon runs roughly parallel to the equator, yet surprisingly the average temperature at Santarém, 400 miles up the river, is only 78 degrees Fahrenheit. In the cooler regions to the south, frosts rarely occur. Altogether, the seasons are a bit lacking in variety. On the other hand, the rainfall varies entirely too much. More than 80 inches falls each year in the Amazon basin, while in the northeast in some places there is almost no rain at all. The state of Ceará is so dry and the sunshine so monotonous that when the sky is overcast the Cearenses greet each other by remarking, "What a beautiful day!"

THE warm climate is still blamed by Brazilians for the country's lack of development and for almost everything else wrong with it. It is held responsible for the "laziness" they regard as their greatest defect (although on occasion laziness is considered an attractive failing too). But what Brazilians call laziness may well be due more to bad health, poor food and boredom than to climate. As more is learned about tropical diseases, nutrition and psychology, and as the lot of the Brazilian poor is improved so that they are healthier and have more to work for, the old-fashioned, moralistic idea of "laziness" may disappear for good.

Most of Brazil lies on a vast, rolling plateau, with only one wave of mountain ranges, which runs north and south, fairly close to the coast. In the north they flatten out to leave the wider coastal plains for sugar-cane raising; in the south they flatten out towards the Uruguay and Paraguay rivers, leaving the vast prairies for cattle raising. But the fairly continuous line of mountains between the coastal plains and the higher, cooler interior has been a great hindrance to the growth of Brazil. The ranges form a barrier that for more than 400 years has helped keep most of the population encamped along the eastern edge of the country as if before a fortress.

ANOTHER big geographical handicap is that although there are great and navigable rivers, they have never served to open up the country or help its economy to any great extent. Brazilians speak enviously of the Mississippi; if only they had had a Mississippi, things would be very different. It is quite true. Large freighters can go 2,300 miles up the Amazon, a river that makes the Mississippi look almost narrow. But the Amazon leads to no vital cities or industrial centers—nor to very many likely sites for such centers. The second most important river, the São Francisco, is similarly navigable, but before it reaches the Atlantic it is interrupted by the falls of Paulo Afonso; and like the Amazon it reaches no important cities. Railroads have been built very slowly. For centuries trade and communications were carried on entirely by coastal shipping, or by mule trains over incredibly bad roads or trails. The air age is changing this state of affairs, and at the same time trunk roads are at last beginning to connect the coastal cities and have started to push into the interior.

Brazil is still more than half covered with forests. It contains, at a rough guess, more than 40,000 plant species, and no one knows how many of these are potentially valuable. As well as all the native and early imported fruit trees like the banana, there are trees that yield rubber, cocoa, Brazil nuts, balsam, resin, fiber, cellulose and tannin. From the palm trees alone come oils and waxes, not to mention dates, coconuts and *palmito,* or hearts of palm.

As far as mineral resources go, the surface has barely been scratched. There is not much coal or oil, but Brazil boasts bauxite, bismuth, barium, asbestos, chromite, columbium, copper, gold, iron (65 billion tons, approximately one third of the world supply), graphite, magnesite, tantalum, lead, limestone, manganese, nickel, diamonds, zinc, radium, titanium, mica, rock crystals, tungsten and atomic ores.

But all this treasure was hidden from the 16th Century explorers and merchants—hidden in the future as well as underground. They kept on risking ships and lives rounding the Cape of Good Hope for spices from the East. From Brazil came only wood and curiosities: dyewood, animals, birds, skins and a few Indians, too.

About 1526, things started to change. The power of Portugal had begun to wane, and its hold on its Far Eastern colonies was soon to weaken. The trip around the Cape of Good Hope was no longer profitable; Portugal discovered that "for every grain of pepper she gave a drop of blood." Furthermore, there were repeated rumors of gold in Brazil. The Portuguese began sending fleets to patrol the coast and fight off the French and the Dutch, who also had designs on the country. A royal agent arrived and serious colonization began.

THE first town to be laid out was São Vicente, now a suburb of Santos, the port of São Paulo. The second was Olinda, far to the northeast; the first arrivals are said to have exclaimed *O! Linda!*—that is, "beautiful"—at the sight of its white, palm-studded beaches. The coast was marked off at intervals of roughly 150 miles, the width of the "captaincies" or land grants which stretched inland. It was in the region around Bahia that sugar first flourished and the plantation system grew up. Negro slaves started arriving from Africa as early as 1535. As the French anthropologist Claude Lévi-Strauss says in *Tristes Tropiques:* "The world, gorged with gold, began to hunger after sugar; and sugar took a lot of slaves." The Indians did not make good slaves; accustomed to life in the forests, they simply gave up and died when set to work in the fields.

In the middle of the 16th Century the French tried twice to settle near what is now Rio, and were twice driven off. After the first expulsion the Portuguese laid out a new town, and after the second victory they named it São Sebastião do Rio de Janeiro, in honor of Saint Sebastian, on whose day the French had been defeated, in the month of January. What had been taken by early explorers to be the mouth of a *rio*, or river, however, was actually only a bay.

The next 250 years repeat a familiar history of European misrule and exploitation of overseas possessions. The period resembles the history of the American colonies under the English, transplanted to a tropical setting and to a Roman Catholic, slaveholding society. Deriving great wealth from Brazil, the Portuguese crown monopolized Brazilian trade. There were unjust taxes and restrictions, yet everything had to be imported from the mother country, since no manufacturing beyond the simplest home industries was allowed. Printing presses were illegal, and so there were no journals or newspapers, and very few books were imported. When gold was at last discovered, it was mined by slave labor and taken under military surveillance straight to the king's treasury.

The Jesuits tried to protect the Indians from slavery in the captaincies. They gathered them into villages, each village organized around a church, converted them and taught them—in other words, "civilized" them. Undoubtedly, the missionaries did save thousands of them from slavery or slaughter, but the Indians died

THE WORLD'S GREATEST RIVER

Cutting across the width of a continent, the Amazon is the undisputed king of rivers. For sheer volume, no river comes close to matching it.

Length: The Amazon is 3,900 miles long. Only the Nile is longer (by 232 miles).
Width: It is five miles wide over long stretches, 40 miles wide downstream.
Volume: Holding 14 times as much water as the Mississippi and 17 times as much as the Nile, it supplies one fifth of all the river water entering the world's oceans.
Tributaries: 500 rivers feed the Amazon, 15 of them more than 1,000 miles long.
Name: Because an explorer saw women warriors along its banks, it was named the Amazon in reference to the mythical realm ruled by women.

off anyway, from smallpox, measles and inanition, and their primitive but unique culture and their skills and arts diminished with them, or blended gradually into the culture of the Portuguese and the Negro slaves.

The first event that could be considered "national," implying some cooperation between the settlements and a sense of identity as a country, was the final driving out of the Protestant Dutch. For 20 years they had controlled the northeast coast, during the same period that they were in possession of the Portuguese African colony of Angola, but they were finally driven out for good in 1654, a triumph for the Catholic Church and for Brazil.

After almost a century of rumors and occasional lucky finds, gold was discovered in good quantity in what is now the state of Minas Gerais (General Mines) in 1698. It was there that the first real development of the interior of Brazil took place, owing almost entirely to the efforts of the famous *bandeirantes.* They came from around São Paulo, most of them descendants of the Portuguese and Indian girls, and they were energetic, cruel and rapacious. They traveled in armed bands, or *bandeiras,* along with their wives, children, cattle and Indian slaves, and they made long treks and savage raids, always looking for gold and more slaves, even attacking and destroying the Jesuit villages and carrying off their own blood brothers into slavery. They penetrated far into the interior, into the present states of Minas Gerais, Goiás and Mato Grosso. They discovered the more glamorous items of Brazil's mineral wealth—diamonds and semiprecious stones as well as gold—and, incidentally, made the young country conscious of its unprecedented size and its forbidding geography.

A small but brilliant constellation of mining towns appeared on the sites of the *bandeirantes'* important finds. The term "mining town" suggests something quite different, however, from these miniature cities—wealthy, isolated outposts of 18th Century culture and rationalism. Vila Rica (now Ouro Prêto) was the capital. Diamantina, now almost unknown outside Brazil, was famous in Europe as the diamond center of the world until the discovery of the Kimberley lodes in Africa in 1870.

IT was in this group of small, flourishing city-towns that an event of great importance in Brazilian history and of particular interest to Americans took place in 1789. It was an abortive, tragic attempt to achieve independence from Portugal, and it goes by the odd name of the *Inconfidência Mineira,* meaning, more or less, the Minas Conspiracy.

The standards of culture and education in these towns were probably higher than in any other part of Brazil at the time, and in addition to mineowners there were many teachers, lawyers and army officers. A group of six of these young men wrote poetry and thought of themselves as a "school." Not only that, but in those barren highlands, glittering with ores, they thought of themselves as "Arcadians," imitating the literary "academies" of Rio and Bahia, that were in turn late imitations of such institutions in Renaissance Italy. The poets took the names of Greek shepherds and wrote long pastoral poems—and epics and satires as well. It seems as though artificiality could not go much further, but there were real talents among them. They were also resentful of Portuguese rule and passionately interested in history and politics. Most particularly they were excited by the recent successful American Revolution, which became their inspiration.

They were joined by other intellectuals and army officers, one of whom became the leader of the movement. He was a lieutenant named Joaquim José da Silva Xavier. Occasionally he practiced dentistry, and so his nickname was "Tiradentes" (Toothpuller). The group corresponded with Thomas Jefferson, and finally in 1787 one of them was sent to meet Jefferson in France, where he was minister plenipotentiary of the newly formed United States. Jefferson, on a trip for his health, cautiously met the Brazilian in the Roman amphitheater at Nîmes. Samuel Putnam, in his book about Brazilian literature called *Marvelous Journey,* says, ". . . this event, although most North Americans have never heard of it, has since become for Brazilians one of the strongest of bonds between their democracy and our own."

Asked his advice about how to foment a revolution and found a republic (and probably about the possibility of American assistance), Jefferson, as a diplomat, could promise nothing more than moral support. The young envoy who talked with him died on the way back to Brazil, but the conspiracy in Minas, perhaps acting under false expectations of American help, went ahead, and grew overbold. The plot was found out, and all the conspirators were drastically punished. Tiradentes himself was hanged and quartered. His house was destroyed and the ground where it had stood was strewn with salt, in the ancient way, to make his house and line, symbolically, barren forever.

THE little "School of Minas," if it can really be called a school, was wiped out, and not only was the first Brazilian movement for independence destroyed but also one of the first attempts at an indigenous literary movement. Brazil's brave but impractical Arcadian poets of 1789 could not arouse their country or do battle themselves like the hardheaded American farmers of 1776. But Tiradentes remains the greatest hero of Brazil. "Toothpuller Day" is a national holiday, and almost every town in Brazil has its Tiradentes Square or Street. As the 18th Century drew to a close, rebellion against Portugal was at least dreamed of—although independence was not to come for 33 more years and then not by means of anything so drastic as revolutionary war.

LEADING a massive ox team that pulls a small cart, a boy treads through a village in Minas Gerais. In rural areas, hitching up a dozen extra oxen is a form of display.

FLOATING on the Rio Negro, the raft-houses lining the city of Manaus are safe against the seasonal floods. Some of the inhabitants ply the river as petty tradesmen.

The Untamed World of a Vast Interior

Journeying from the coast of Brazil to the farthest interior is like taking a trip through zones of increasing desolation. In the near hinterland, quiet towns, landed estates and workers' huts dot the hillsides. Men have been here for centuries, clearing the forests and planting crops. Beyond is the scrubland of the cattlemen, a shifting frontier whose inhabitants are fiercely independent and often violent. Where the rainfall is heavy, the Amazon forest rises, inhuman and repellent, an appendage of wilderness occupying almost half the area of Brazil.

AWESOME RIVERS roll ponderously through remote forests, generating power still largely untapped by industry

COILING through the green jungle below Manaus (*opposite*), the Amazon pours into numerous channels to create vast swamps.

CASCADING down a long jagged row of cliffs, the waters of the Iguassú River drop into a narrow gorge some 210 feet below.

ON A TRAIL in the Mato Grosso forest, a Camayurá warrior carries his child (*opposite*). Most of Brazil's 800,000 Indians live mainly on fish and cassava meal.

IN A HAMMOCK, a device invented by South American Indians, sit two stoical members of the Auiti tribe. Simple ailments like the cold have decimated the Indians.

EASY COMRADESHIP exists between the Indians and Orlando Villas Boas (*above*), who spends his life screening Mato Grosso tribes from white men's guns and diseases.

JUNGLE VICTIM is evidenced by a white man's skull found by Villas Boas (*opposite*). He tries to maintain peace by moving tribes away when white settlers arrive.

38

On a visit to Niagara Falls in 1876, a bewhiskered Dom Pedro II, Emperor of Brazil, looks like a model Victorian as he sits with

his wife and entourage. His 58-year reign was notably peaceful.

3

Century of Honor and Pride

THE history of South America in the 19th Century resembles Shakespeare's battle scenes: alarums and trumpets; small armies on-stage, small armies off-stage; bloodshed, death scenes and pauses in the action for fine speeches. But Brazil differed from the rest of the continent in two ways. First, while all the other South American colonies rebelled against Spanish rule and finally formed themselves into nine republics, Brazil, while becoming independent of Portugal, remained politically united. It had minor civil wars and secessions, some lasting several years, but it always pulled itself together again. And second, it had no real war of independence. It was ruled by the Portuguese House of Braganza until 1889, and it still has a Braganza pretender to the throne —rather, it has two pretenders, first cousins.

The long period of relative stability gave the country great advantages: a strong feeling of national unity and almost a century of history in which it still takes pride. But the pride is tinged with nostalgia, and sometimes even with bitterness. Brazilians feel that their national honor, international reputation and foreign credit—and even the size and prestige of their navy—have never since stood so high.

MODERN Brazilian history begins with Napoleon. The world remembers him for having created an empire in the first years of the 19th Century and for having himself crowned Emperor of France. But few people realize that as a by-product of the Napoleonic Empire the Empire of Brazil was also created, and lasted much longer than Napoleon's—67 years, to be exact. This was a remarkably long time to have held out in the 19th Century, when revolutions were crashing like thunderstorms in neighboring countries, and when the forces of liberalism, equalitarianism and republicanism were constantly growing stronger and more articulate throughout the western world.

There were groups within the new countries of the Western Hemisphere that felt a monarchy was still the best and most stable form of government. After the Revolutionary War the United States had had a small movement to make George Washington a king, and Argentina during its own revolutionary period in the early 19th Century had shopped around for a suitable European prince. The experiment was tried in Mexico in the 1860s with Maximilian, and failed dismally. But in the paradoxical way things often seem to happen in Brazil, what brought the country eventual political independence from Portugal was the arrival of the Portuguese royal family.

In 1807 Napoleon was trying to force Portugal to join his alliance against England, and his armies were closing in on Lisbon. Maria I, the Portuguese queen, had long been insane, and her son, Dom João, was regent. Portugal had been almost an economic protectorate of England for a hundred years. Caught, as the American historian C. H. Haring puts it, "between the military imperialism of Napoleon and the economic imperialism of Great Britain," Dom João, never decisive at best, shilly-shallied. At the last possible moment he settled for Great Britain. Then, prompted by the British and anxious to save his throne, he decided to move the whole royal family and court to Brazil.

It was one of the strangest hegiras in history. In a state of near panic, the mad queen, Dom João, his estranged wife, their children and the entire Portuguese court—about 15,000 people —were squeezed aboard some 40 merchant vessels. With a British escort they took off for Brazil, the unknown, romantic colony where most of their wealth—and sugar—came from. The voyage was a nightmare of storms, seasickness, short rations and stinking water. The courtiers complained so much that a royal command was issued that "only nautical subjects" were to be discussed. Meanwhile, Pedro, the nine-year-old heir apparent, discoursed learnedly on Virgil's *Aeneid* with his tutors, supposedly comparing his father's plight to that of Aeneas. However, as Octavio Tarquinio de Sousa, the well-known Brazilian historian of the Empire period, says: "Dom João saved the dynasty, and took with him intact the greatest treasures of the kingdom, including art, jewels, and books [60,000 of them, the nucleus of Brazil's present National Library] to the lands where he would found a great empire."

AFTER 52 hideous days they reached Bahia, and were received with wild rejoicing. The story goes that poor distracted Queen Maria, seeing Negroes prancing around her sedan chair, thought that she was in hell and screamed that the devils were after her. After a month they went on to Rio, to equally great celebrations. Already Dom João had issued a Royal Letter declaring the ports of Brazil open to all friendly nations, by which he meant chiefly England. He also won popularity by establishing a printing press; the iron industry was begun and the textile industry expanded. The arts and sciences were encouraged. Almost overnight Brazil felt itself changing from an exploited colony to an independent power.

Rio was a hot, squalid city of about 60,000 inhabitants, without a sewage system or water works. The royal family, oddly enough, settled down and began to like its new home and the country's easygoing ways. But the court in general hated everything, and was hated in return by the Brazilians—a reaction that was to have serious political consequences. Housing and carriages were scarce; the food was bad; the ladies and gentlemen of the transported court were scared of tropical diseases, and of the thunderstorms that bounced from peak to peak around the bay.

BUT the 13-year stay of a sophisticated European court changed Rio into the nation's capital and changed the state of affairs in much of Brazil. The administration of justice was somewhat improved; the first bank was founded; and the naval academy and schools of medicine and surgery were established, as well as a library and the Botanical Garden. In 1814, with Napoleon defeated, Portugal was rid of the threat from France, and in 1816 Dom João invited a French mission of architects, musicians, painters and sculptors to visit Brazil. He started building a royal palace on the outskirts of the city. Finally the mad queen died and her son, Dom João, became João VI of Portugal and Brazil.

But by 1820 the liberal forces in Portugal made it necessary for Dom João to return if he wanted to save his throne. Again he shilly-shallied, partly because of his love for Brazil, and partly because he could not face that ocean voyage a second time. He granted two new constitutions, one for Portugal and one for Brazil, and then—at the urging of the British—sailed away. Before he left he had a conversation with the heir apparent, Dom Pedro, in which he prophesied the secession of Brazil from Portugal and advised his son to take the crown for himself. He also cleaned out the Bank of Brazil and took with him all the jewels he could collect.

His departure was the first of several Brazilian abdications or "renunciations" of power, which are often discussed in terms of João VI's unhappy career. Not all of the abdicators have filled their pockets as liberally as he did, and their reasons for leaving have varied, but this was the first occurrence of what has become a peculiarly Brazilian phenomenon.

Dom Pedro had been badly brought up. He had led the luxurious but slovenly life of the small upper class of Brazilians of his day; he had been friendly with slaves and stableboys, and from his teens his love affairs were notorious. A fascinating character, he was a brilliant, energetic, spoiled and dissipated neurotic. He suffered from occasional epileptic fits. He was fundamentally kindhearted, generous toward his mistresses and devoted to his children, legitimate and illegitimate alike. He wanted to be a good ruler. But the court was still mostly Portuguese and still unpopular among the Brazilians. Dom Pedro relied on it, and things started to go badly for him almost immediately.

Not long after Dom João had left for Lisbon, the Portuguese government began issuing orders restoring some of the old colonial restrictions. An order came for Dom Pedro to return to Portugal immediately to finish his education. While he was on a trip to São Paulo, further high-handed orders arrived, and were delivered to him as he sat on his horse on the bank of a little stream, the Ipiranga. Dom Pedro read the orders, waved his saber in the air and shouted "Independence or death!" This was the famous *Grito*, or Cry, of Ipiranga, and the day on which Dom Pedro gave it, September 7th, is the Brazilian Fourth of July.

DOM PEDRO was proclaimed emperor of an independent Brazil. He reigned only nine years, however. He considered himself a liberal, and an advanced one, and the constitution that he granted in 1824 lasted until the end of the monarchy. But there were constant revolts, mercenary soldiers made trouble, regional differences and needs were not recognized, and the Emperor's private life became too scandalous for even the tolerant Brazilians.

After João VI's death Dom Pedro became heir to the throne of Portugal. He conceded the crown to his daughter, Maria da Glória, but his own younger brother, Miguel, was in Vienna and soon arrived in Portugal to try to take power. Rebellions broke out all over Brazil. Dom Pedro's personal army deserted him. Then he, too, abdicated the throne, leaving for Europe to fight for his daughter's right to the Portuguese throne.

Dom Pedro I had been a high-minded ruler, very much superior to João VI and well intentioned. Ruling Brazil had been beyond his powers. And the ruler that Dom Pedro left behind him was only five years old.

EXCEPT that he proved to be equally energetic, Dom Pedro II was almost exactly the opposite of his mercurial, dissipated father. He was carefully, even overcarefully educated by a beloved governess and a series of tutors. He grew up to be serious, hard-working and cultivated, and for 49 years he did his very best to govern his country.

Dom Pedro II was not a genius, but he was a remarkable man for a member of the Braganza line, and in most respects he was much in advance of his countrymen. He was an imposing Emperor: six feet four inches tall, with blue eyes inherited from his German mother and a large bushy beard that early turned white. He himself felt that he was better fitted for an intellectual life than a political one, but always he did his duty. The government was monarchial, constitutional and representative, and the laws were made by two parliamentary houses. Roman Catholicism was the state religion, but religious freedom was guaranteed, as well as freedom of speech and of the press. There was taxation according to wealth. Dom Pedro's chief strength was his "moderating power," under which he could dismiss almost anyone he wanted to, prorogue Congress or dissolve the Chamber of Deputies if he thought the state of the country warranted it.

According to the more liberal-minded ministers, he abused his "moderating power" and changed the government too often, particularly in the early years of his reign. But as he grew older he grew more patient and more liberal.

He never took political revenge. He appointed men for their good qualities, no matter what their loyalties were, and Brazil has seldom had men of such high caliber in public office since. However, he greatly underestimated the growing commercial and business interests of his country, and he always favored the old landowning aristocracy.

After 30 years of rule, Dom Pedro II at last permitted himself to go abroad. He visited Europe and later the United States, and subsequently made longer trips to Europe, Egypt and the Holy Land. During his travels his older daughter, the heiress apparent Princess Isabel, acted as regent. He traveled incognito, as Dom Pedro de Alcântara, and his democratic ways, gift for languages, good humor and boundless energy made him "the most popular royal person in Europe." He sought out literary leaders wherever he went and talked to them in their own languages. Victor Hugo called him "a grandson of Marcus Aurelius." He was fascinated by comparative religions (which shocked his more devout subjects), and made a point of visiting synagogues and reading aloud in Hebrew.

IN 1876 he paid a long visit to the United States. He had read the Boston Transcendentalists and Abolitionists and had corresponded with John Greenleaf Whittier, one of whose poems he translated into Portuguese. It was called "The Cry of a Lost Soul." When he met Whittier, Dom Pedro startled the shy Quaker poet by attempting to give him the Brazilian *abraço,* or hug. He also met Henry Wadsworth Longfellow, who gave a dinner party for him and subsequently described his royal guest as a "modern Haroun-al-Raschid wandering about to see the great world as a simple traveller, not as a king. He is a hearty, genial, noble person, very liberal in his views."

A photograph exists of the royal party taken on its visit to Niagara Falls. There is something sad, even tragic about this foreign-looking group paying the conventional visit to the conventional "sights" and having its picture taken. The situation is somehow symbolic of late 19th Century Brazil. The eagerly grasped-at foreign influences, the attempt to adopt the inappropriate and the neglect or ignorance of resources at home—the old photograph suggests all of these. Dom Pedro was the owner, so to speak, of a waterfall even higher than Niagara and almost as spectacular, but few people in Brazil paid very much attention to it.

Nevertheless, it was during Dom Pedro's long reign that Brazil's material expansion really began. In 1850 a Commercial Code was issued that, with additions, has remained in force to this day. More banks were established, and foreign capital (still mostly British) began to enter. In 1854 the first railroad started off toward Petrópolis, the Emperor's favorite place of residence. Gaslights were installed in the Rio streets. Other short railroads were built, although transportation was one of the country's biggest problems, as it still is today.

Progress was slow, partly because of the favoritism shown by Dom Pedro to the landed aristocracy, who were usually conservative and indifferent to "modern improvements" and who looked down on the new class of merchants and bankers. The towns were still inhabited mostly by artisans and Portuguese merchants; the aristocracy lived on their *fazendas* and much preferred to go to Paris, when they could afford to. Dom Pedro created many titles, principally baronies. Most of the new barons were landed proprietors who had grown rich on sugar or coffee—for by this time coffee was the leading crop and Brazil was supplying the world. One exception was Irineo Evangelista de Sousa, the

POPULAR TOURIST, Emperor Dom Pedro II doffs his hat to New Yorkers after completing his 9,000-mile trip through the U.S. in 1876.

Baron Mauá, later Viscount Mauá, who was the J. P. Morgan of Brazil. Some of his many activities are reflected in his extraordinary coat of arms, which showed a steamship, a locomotive and four lampposts (like ones he had installed in Rio). Mauá was an associate of the great Rothschild family and part-owner of banks in London, New York, Uruguay and Argentina. His career marks the transition in Brazil from the agricultural economy of the plantation world to the world of modern, expanding capitalism.

There had been two foreign wars, the first undertaken in 1851-1852 partly to get rid of the brutal Rosas regime in Argentina. The second was Brazil's one real war, fought against Paraguay. It lasted from 1865 to 1870 and is still regarded by Brazilians with a mixture of pride and shame. Its beginnings were complicated, having to do with the rights of Brazilian citizens in Uruguay, and it was urged on the nation by the always more warlike states of the south. Paraguay was ruined by the war. But even though Argentina and Uruguay had been Brazil's allies during the conflict, the war debt incurred by Brazil hung over Dom Pedro for the rest of his reign.

The biggest problem of Dom Pedro's reign, however, and probably of his own personal life, was slavery. So closely was slavery bound up with the Empire and the Emperor that the end of the monarchy and the death of Dom Pedro both followed soon after emancipation. The Emperor loathed slavery, believing it to be a shameful blot on his beautiful, beloved country, and he liberated all his own inherited slaves as early as 1840. But he also thought that emancipation would have to come gradually in the country as a whole in order not to upset the economy, which during his reign was dependent almost entirely on slave labor.

Back in 1826, in return for recognition of the Brazilian Empire and for certain trade treaties, Dom Pedro I had made a bargain with England: the slave trade was to stop by 1830. But thousands of slaves continued to be smuggled into the country every year, and this was a constant source of trouble with the English. Over the years, laws leading to emancipation were urged: they were usually agitated for by the Liberals and then actually passed only when a Conservative government again came into power. The law of the *Ventre Livre* provided that all children born of slaves after 1871 would be free, as well as all slaves that still belonged to the crown or to the state. The next step, in 1885, was the passing of a law that all slaves were to be free when they reached the age of 60. São Paulo freed all slaves within the city; various states began freeing them, and the army began to protest against orders to pursue runaway slaves.

The institution was obviously doomed, but the landed proprietors in general did nothing to provide for a future without slave labor. There had been sporadic attempts to encourage immigration. But, as C. H. Haring says, it was hard to get workers to come to a country "where agricultural labor was equated with human slavery."

IN 1887 Dom Pedro again went to Europe, leaving Princess Isabel as regent. He was exhausted and diabetic and looked far older than his age. Isabel had always been an abolitionist and now, partly by her own wish and partly under pressure from the abolitionists, she signed the emancipation proclamation. The day was May 13, 1888. There was a week of celebration.

However, the act ruined most of the rich planters, and 300 million dollars' worth of property was made valueless. Naturally, many of the landowners turned against the monarchy and joined the growing republican movement.

There was also widespread suspicion of Isabel's husband, the French Count d'Eu. The Brazilians were afraid of foreign influence. Isabel herself was none too popular, and even those devoted to the old Emperor felt dubious about a woman's succeeding to the throne. The republican movement was led by Benjamin Constant Botelho de Magalhães, who was inspired by the dry doctrines of Auguste Comte, the French philosopher whose Positivist beliefs had taken a strong hold on intellectual Brazilians.

THE end of the monarchy came very suddenly and was a complete surprise to most of the nation. The Emperor returned and received a great welcome. But Benjamin Constant and Marshal Floriano Peixoto, who represented disaffected elements in the army, engineered a military revolt, involving Marshal Deodoro da Fonseca (who had been a devoted follower of the Emperor), and on November 15th, 1889, the Republic of Brazil was proclaimed. The Emperor left by ship on a rainy night with all his family, a few friends and his doctor. He was offered a large sum of money but, impeccable and dignified to the end, refused it. His empress died shortly after, but he lived on for two more years, mostly in France, quietly going on with his studies of Tupi, Hebrew, Arabic and Sanskrit. He was never heard to say a bitter word against his political enemies.

In many ways Dom Pedro failed to accomplish much. Brazil was still almost empty, almost completely illiterate and divided between the few very rich and the many miserably poor. In spite of the Emperor's respect for education no universities had been founded. Enrollments in schools of higher education were small and the teaching was inferior.

However, Brazil had changed from an 18th Century, monarchial, slaveholding, primitive agricultural country to a republic free of slaves, newly prosperous from its coffee trade and aware of the outside world. Dom Pedro achieved only a small part of his dreams for Brazil—but if there were more monarchs like him, world history would make more edifying reading.

A trio of patricians, Senhora Bulhões de Carvalho da Fonseca and her children are part of the inner circle of the aristocracy.

A Short-lived Empire's Surviving Elite

Although the Empire and most of the patriarchal plantations have long since passed away, the aristocratic past lingers on in Brazil's republic. Two pretenders to the nonexistent imperial throne are well-known society figures today. There are still families who value large landed estates more highly than great fortunes in steel. In the midst of democracy and modern commerce, Brazil's aristocrats maintain old traditions of public service and polished elegance.

UNIFORMED BUTLER serves coffee at a Portuguese-style mansion (*left*) set in Rio's hills. Homes like this were designed to serve the needs of large patriarchal families.

TURF FANCIERS at the Rio Jockey Club track include gold-braided officers (*opposite*). At the running of the *Grande Premio Brasil*, the elite turns up in full force.

OPEN RANKS *of the upper class include men in government*

and other professions as well as old landed families

FORMAL RECEPTION brings members of the diplomatic corps and their wives to a palace in Rio to greet a foreign dignitary.

GLITTERING FETE is attended by visitors to Petrópolis (*right*), a summer resort for socialites and tourists 60 miles from Rio.

Brazil's first capital, Bahia, looks much as it did two centuries ago when it was the palmy center of the sugar boom. No longer so

prosperous, the 400-year-old city remains festive and easygoing.

4

Shifting Centers for Government

BRAZIL has had three capitals—Bahia, Rio de Janeiro and, since 1960, the new city of Brasília. The seat of the government has been moved geographically as the country itself has changed historically and economically. The change from Bahia to Rio was a logical one, suggested by the country's growth. The recent change from Rio to Brasília is as much a gesture of hope as a reaction to necessity; it is an idealistic approach to the old problems of opening up the interior and securing a more efficient government.

Bahia, or Salvador, was appropriately enough the first capital, since the country had its beginnings in the state of Bahia. The *bahia*, or bay, was discovered in 1501 by a Portuguese expedition whose navigator was Amerigo Vespucci (the man after whom the American continents were named), and later the comprehensive name of *São Salvador da Bahia de Todos os Santos* (Holy Savior of the Bay of All Saints) was given to it. In 1534 the first captaincy was

53

established, a small group of thatched huts inside a stockade. This was very soon attacked and destroyed by Indians—who also ate some of the unhappy adventurers.

The first governor general of Brazil, Thomé de Souza, arrived in 1549 with several hundred soldiers and Portuguese exiles and orders from the king to establish a "large and strong settlement" that would serve as capital of the new country. For the sake of defense the new city was built on the heights overlooking the sea, more like a fort than a town. Besides the Portuguese, the first inhabitants were principally "pacified" Indians.

The town grew so quickly that it overflowed the walls and descended to the seashore, creating the higher and lower towns that still exist. Protected by the viceroys of the Portuguese crown and growing fabulously rich during the sugar boom of the 17th and 18th Centuries, Bahia was also the biggest port of entry for Negro slaves. These came from many African nations and from every level of culture. Some of them were educated Mohammedans; occasionally, it is said, they even taught their masters how to read and write. There were slaves skilled in iron working, cattle raising and cooking; there were skilled musicians, and others who knew how to cultivate the banana and the palm.

THE fact that the capital was transferred to Rio de Janeiro in 1763 is one reason Bahia has preserved its colonial character so well. It remained rich and important for many years, but when it ceased to be the capital, building on a large scale stopped. By the time the wave of modern building hit Bahia, the city's old buildings were regarded as sacred; protected by centuries of traditions, they were spared destruction. Today, although Bahia continues to grow and build and modernize, the old part of the city remains almost unchanged and dominates the newer sections.

Bahianos are extremely proud of their city; they call it "the good place." The Cariocas of Rio, referring to the large numbers of Bahianos who come south to their city every year, ironically add: "Yes, Bahia's the good place—it there, and me here!"

Bahia is often the first Brazilian city seen by travelers approaching by sea, and the huge port with its busy waterfront life, heat, pungent smells and large Negro population makes a strong and lasting impression. Its ancient forts on the ocean, its magnificent if moldering baroque buildings, its black and white crowds, frequent religious processions, street vendors, open-air restaurants and markets, where the best folk art in Brazil is for sale—all combine to make it seem "typically Brazilian."

BAHIA'S African-influenced cooking is particularly famous, making use of *dendé* palm oil, fresh ginger, dried shrimps, coconut milk and dozens of other exotic ingredients. The costume of the city's Negro and mulatto women is reminiscent of colonial styles. It consists of a full, printed skirt, a loose white chemise (usually made of homespun cotton) trimmed with handmade lace, a turban, earrings, necklaces and sometimes, at the waist, a *balangandã*, a jangling collection of silver charms on a silver loop. In the old days the *balangandãs* were sometimes made of gold, and the wealth of a slave's owner was shown by the jewelry which the slave wore. Today Bahianas—women from Bahia dressed in this costume—are often street vendors. With their portable foodstands and little charcoal braziers, they are familiar figures in São Paulo, Rio and other cities. They sell coconut candy, heavy cakes of tapioca, mysterious confections wrapped in corn husks, broiled corn on the cob and other specialties of the north.

Bahia presents a constant succession of *festas* and pilgrimages. Famous all over Brazil is the annual festival of the *Senhor do Bonfim* (Lord of the Good End). Not only the Negro population and the poor people trek to the Bonfim; statesmen, politicians, generals and millionaires alike can be seen in the processions, carrying lighted candles as they move toward the famous little 18th Century church that is the object of the pilgrimage.

With its large Negro population, Bahia is the center of *candomblé*, that highly developed, intensely emotional mixture of African cults and Roman Catholicism which in other Brazilian cities is known as *macumba*. Bahianos also practice the art of *capoeira*, a form of combined wrestling and jujitsu in which only the feet are used. It is lightning quick and graceful —another importation from Africa.

Bahia was built specifically to be a capital, but the origins of Rio de Janeiro were more haphazard. The first colony was established in 1555 on the magnificent Bay of Guanabara by a group of French Huguenots, without as much as a by-your-leave to the Portuguese. Because it was so far south of Europe the settlement called itself, ambitiously, "Antarctic France," and its leader was Nicolas Durand de Villegaignon, a religious tyrant who dreamed of founding a Utopia there.

To expel the French, who were allied with the Indians, the governor general in Bahia sent his nephew Estácio de Sá 800 miles to the south. In the battle that brought the Portuguese victory over the French, Estácio, "a boy of gentle presence," was killed by an Indian arrow in the face, thereby becoming a kind of lay-patron of the city—as St. Sebastian is the patron saint. For reasons of defense, the Portuguese settlement moved to the Morro do Castelo (Fortress Hill), and it was there that the colonial town of Rio grew up.

WHEN the Portuguese court arrived in 1808, Rio was still only a squalid colonial village. The viceroy and his council quickly solved the housing problem of those days: the quartermasters requisitioned the best houses for the gentlemen of the court. A bailiff gave an eviction notice simply by painting the letters P.R. (for Prince Regent) on the doors of the houses needed. The Cariocas translated the letters in their own way as *Ponha-se na rua*— "Get out in the street"—and that was that.

The city made progress all through the Empire period, but the biggest time of growth came after the consolidation of the republic.

In the euphoric period before World War I it started taking on its present appearance. The mayors at that time destroyed many ancient streets and alleyways—and unfortunately, along with them, many irreplaceable old buildings, plazas and fountains. They flattened out hills, filled in stretches of the bay and opened up avenues. They built the long line of docks and the handsome brick warehouses where the black stevedores today work, wearing only ragged shorts and straw hats. The cable cars to the top of the familiar Sugar Loaf Mountain date from this period, as does the little funicular railway that ascends to the peak of the Corcovado (Hunchback). Between 1930 and 1960, the outlying section of Copacabana grew from little more than a suburb, with a half-deserted beach, to the currently overpopulated "south zone" with its 10-story-high apartment houses. The 100-foot-tall figure of Christ the Redeemer by French Sculptor Paul Landowski was placed on top of the Corcovado in 1931 to commemorate the first century of Brazilian political independence.

BECAUSE of the extravagant outcroppings of rocks and mountains at its back and the marshes and swamps flanking it, Rio developed as an isolated city in spite of its size, and its problems of housing and transportation have always been formidable. There is only one highway leading from Rio into the interior; within the city itself the main streets and avenues either cut between or tunnel under the mountains, or run along the bay on filled-in land. Many of the old squares and plazas were originally lagoons or swamps. The city could not expand along the coast because the malarial mosquito made the surrounding marshes uninhabitable. Now, however, modern sanitation has changed that, and enormous suburbs have spread out to the north and northwest.

The topography of Rio is fantastically beautiful, but it defies any kind of systematic city planning. The city has penetrated like the fingers of a hand between the granite peaks and the precipitous conical hills. Although poor people have always lived on the *morros,* it is only during the last 20 years or so that these hills have become covered with the groups of shacks called *favelas,* most of which are inhabited by immigrants from the northeast of Brazil. It is roughly estimated that 700,000 of Rio's 3.3 million inhabitants now live in these slums, thereby creating the worst of the city's many problems.

The thousands upon thousands of shacks pile up against the hills, or stretch out to the north over the filled land to the city's dumps. *Urubus,* or vultures, their only scavengers, hover over them. The shacks have no sanitation or running water; all day the women and children stand in line at the few spigots provided, to fill old oil cans with city water—which at that often fails. The *favelas* are natural breeding grounds for disease, crime and social unrest. Nevertheless, as soon as a housing project draws a thousand or so *favela* dwellers to better quarters, the same number of immigrants from the northeast mysteriously appears, ready to move into the vacated shacks.

For there is no denying the attractions which city life, even at its worst, holds for these people. In the small towns or villages of the interior there is the same poverty, plus boredom and isolation. In the city there are the bright lights, radio and television (it is surprising how many antennas appear above the *favela* shacks), *futebol* (soccer football), the lotteries, the constant excitement and the sense of participation—even if only on the lowest level—in the life of a great city. All this offsets the misery and filth, the standing in line for water and the frequent visits of the police.

RIO is a city of surprises. A busy street turns into an endless flight of steep steps. The Santos Dumont Airport—for small planes—is near the center of town. Right at the end of Avenida Rio Branco, the principal street, a gigantic ocean liner may loom up. Old buildings and even hills are continually being removed to make way for new structures and new developments, and although the limits of the colonial

town are still indicated by the oldest churches and other public buildings, the Morro do Castelo itself was cleared away in 1922 in one of those scene-shifting operations that are characteristic of the city and astonishing to the visitor. "What has happened to Rio?" invariably asks the Carioca who has been away for two or three years. One who had been away for 12 years had to buy a map of the city before he could find his way around the business section of his home town again.

Upper-class dwellers on the upper floors of apartment houses often look straight into *favelas* only a few yards away. Sometimes the intimacy can be chaotic. A couple returning one night to their eighth-floor apartment on the Morro da Viuva (Widow's Hill) heard a terrific bumping and crashing going on inside and naturally thought, "Burglars!" But when they opened the door they found only a panic-stricken horse in the living room. So close are the buildings to the peaks and slabs of native rock and vegetation that the horse had managed to fall from his oblique, minute pasture straight onto their terrace.

TODAY Rio is no longer the capital of the country. The actual drive to move the seat of government to the interior began in 1956, but the idea of establishing such a utopian capital city had existed for more than a century. The move was thought of as a sort of exodus to a land of Canaan, a great stroke that would solve the country's problems as if by magic. A capital in the interior would be a romantic repetition of the long marches of the *bandeirantes* through the wilderness, bringing civilization to the remotest areas, as far away as the western frontier. It was the myth of the city of gold, with the possibility of wealth and opportunity for all. On a more mundane level, a central capital would offer better living conditions and fewer distractions for government workers, and it would help to develop those great empty spaces that have haunted Brazil for so long.

One of the earliest leaders to dream of a central capital was José Bonifácio, adviser to

Dom Pedro I in the 1820s. Bonifácio may even be responsible for the name "Brasília." In the middle of the 19th Century, the Brazilian historian Francisco Adolfo de Varnhagen argued for a capital which would be at an imaginary meeting point of the principal drainage systems of Brazil—of the Amazon, Paraná and São Francisco Rivers. Varnhagen's imaginary city was to be more or less where Brasília now is. The first constitution under the Republic, in 1891, specified the marking out of a quadrilateral on the central plateau of Brazil where the future Federal District was to be situated. After the Vargas dictatorship ended in 1945, a new constitution called for the transfer of the capital to a conveniently located city within the prescribed quadrilateral in the state of Goías, and ordered that a commission be formed to prepare for the change. Every opportunistic journalist, every political candidate looking for popularity denounced as "crabs" those who wanted to cling to the coast and keep on ignoring the fertile interior.

When President Juscelino Kubitschek came into office in 1956, he wanted to distinguish his term by a never-to-be-forgotten public work. One of his first acts as president was to announce that the capital long dreamed of was to be built at last, and an enabling act was passed by both legislative houses almost without objection. As a site for the capital, the government decided on a bleak, almost barren plain where Brasília is now.

IT is of course to Kubitschek's credit that he had remarkably sophisticated tastes in architecture for a head of state. The world-famous Brazilian architect Oscar Niemeyer had for many years been a close friend of his and had previously designed buildings for him, and now Niemeyer was commissioned to design all the government buildings in the new capital. All other buildings had to have his approval. The site plan, giving the city the shape of an airplane or bird, was by Niemeyer's friend and onetime teacher Lúcio Costa, the dean of Brazilian architects.

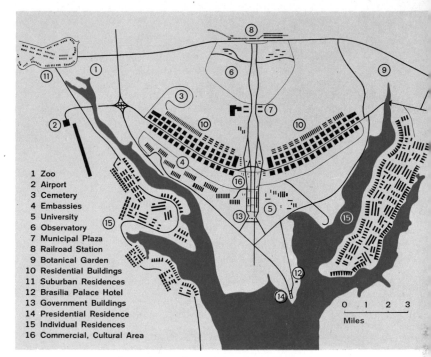

1 Zoo
2 Airport
3 Cemetery
4 Embassies
5 University
6 Observatory
7 Municipal Plaza
8 Railroad Station
9 Botanical Garden
10 Residential Buildings
11 Suburban Residences
12 Brasília Palace Hotel
13 Government Buildings
14 Presidential Residence
15 Individual Residences
16 Commercial, Cultural Area

AIRPLANE SHAPE of Brasília is formed by the crossing of two main axes. The fuselage is the four-mile mall running from the Municipal Plaza (7) to the government buildings (13). The swept-back wings comprise two apartment house districts (10). Where the axes cross are the shops and amusements of "downtown" Brasília.

There was no railroad to the site and only dirt roads. The Brazilian economy was already in a bad way, but Kubitschek embarked on his monumental plan anyway, and construction was begun. Much of the building material had to be flown in—at staggering cost. A sprawling, ramshackle shantytown, the "Free City" for immigrant workers, grew up near the site. Difficulties arose immediately, but Kubitschek —optimistic, energetic and ebullient—refused to acknowledge them. Amid great fanfare the government was officially installed in the new capital in April 1960.

The legislators and members of some executive ministries are now required by law to live there, at least part time, but Brasília is still only partly finished. Construction on many buildings has stopped, and it is hard to say when the country will be able to start large-scale building again. To date it has cost the Brazilian people more than 600 million dollars, magnifying the country's economic emergency.

The results of all this expenditure and of three years of round-the-clock work are controversial, to say the least. That it got built—as much of it as is built—was an undeniable feat of energy and determination. Individual buildings are very beautiful, but the city as a whole leaves much to be desired esthetically. There is little feeling of scale; the buildings are lost in the surrounding vastness, and even within the city limits the sensation of being on another planet—as everyone puts it—is overwhelming.

Some of the government buildings are too small and annexes have been added, or will have to be. The living quarters for the president's servants, and for those working in Brasília's first big hotel, are both underground. The "superblocks" of apartment houses that photograph so well have some good features, such as their own swimming pools and playgrounds, but are nevertheless as cramped as those in Rio, although set in apparently infinite space.

The city has been laid out to avoid intersections and traffic lights. Entirely dependent on electric power for its elevators and on gasoline for its cars, it is a city built for the automobile, where almost nothing can be reached on foot. Because it ignores the pedestrian, the stroller and the café-sitter, and provides few possibilities for neighborhood life or plaza life, Brasília has been called an "old-fashioned" city, and is considered at least 35 years behind the times by some contemporary city-planners.

IT may be too early to judge Brasília from a practical point of view, but the evidence to date is not encouraging. The isolated city is a difficult place to govern from, and legislators so dislike going there that it has often been difficult to achieve a quorum in the chamber. Senators and Deputies fight for places on the planes leaving each weekend for Rio or São Paulo. The course of justice in the federal courts has slowed almost to a standstill, and government business has also slowed down woefully. It is even possible to put some of the blame for the sudden departure of President Jânio Quadros in 1961 (see Chapter 9) on Brasília. Never a man at ease with himself or his co-workers, Quadros seemed to feel isolated in the new capital. "Cursed city!" he called it the day he left.

Another disadvantage to Brasília that will be felt for a long time is in the caliber of the men it is drawing to politics. Formerly these were men who felt the attractions of Rio as a place to educate their children, to be in touch with what was going on culturally, to escape from the provincialism of the more remote parts of the country. But now, some people feel, such men will not be attracted to Brasília.

Meanwhile the controversy continues. But whatever the merits and demerits of Brasília, the country is in effect stuck with it, and today few candidates for public office speak against it, publicly at least.

WHAT will become of Rio now that the capital has been changed to Brasília? Opinions vary. The pessimists prophesy poverty and decay: at best, they say, Rio will turn into a historical museum, living on memories of the past and dependent on the tourist trade. Going to the other extreme, the optimists believe that the city, rid of the excess population it has attracted as the capital of the country, will actually improve. They say that without the thousands of government workers Rio will function better than it does at present. Its position as the best loved of Brazilian cities and the cultural capital of the country, the natural gaiety of the Cariocas, Carnival, the beaches—all of its charms and advantages will remain unchanged in spite of dire financial problems, lack of water, inadequate transportation and other civic ills.

So far, Rio gives no sign of realizing that it is no longer the capital. The Cariocas—and almost all Brazilians are potential Cariocas—conceal their jealousy toward Brasília, if they feel any, and laugh at the tribulations of those who have to go there. The fact is that no one is really yet accustomed to the idea of the new capital. Rio continues to be the heart and soul of the country.

At ceremonies marking the opening of Brasília in April 1960, spotlights blaze on the sleek, colonnaded Supreme Court building.

A Frontier Capital's Jet-Age Splendors

The planting of Brasília in the wilderness is not so much a new beginning as it is an historic culmination. For centuries the beckoning hinterlands have been entered many times and hopefully settled many times. Scores of bonanza towns have been planted in the wilds. The city of Manaus on the Amazon sprang up on profits in rubber; Ouro Prêto was created by an 18th Century gold rush. Other towns rotted and died, for Brazilian pioneering has always been unsteady. It has taken the form of sporadic forays which opened new land but left old settlements half empty. In this long story Brasília is the latest chapter, another hopeful plunge into the interior, only more colossal and more splendid than any that went before.

59

HAND LABORER cleans the broad marble roof of a new building in Brasília (*left*). Some 60,000 men worked on a round-the-clock schedule to build the new capital.

SOARING SLABS rising 25 stories above the plain (*opposite*) provide a target for tropical lightning. The two connected towers house the offices for the congressmen.

METROPOLITAN MAZE of apartment houses for government employees (*above*) is arranged geometrically in superblocks which form self-contained communities.

GRACEFUL PILLARS faced with marble flare out from the presidential offices (*below*). Set on columns, many of the capital's buildings seem to float lightly above the ground.

SWIRLING RAMP in the presidential office building glides gently down from a mezzanine to the tiled floor (*below*). In the polished interiors of Brasília's key buildings, architect Oscar Niemeyer made striking use of ramps, split levels and glass to emphasize space and movement —apt themes for a city designed to open a wilderness.

CONICAL CATHEDRAL, 108 feet high and 197 feet in diameter, has a spidery frame of concrete slanting beams. In the completed structure the beams support glass walls.

PLAYFUL FORMS, cast in bronze, represent women washing their hair in the sun (*left*). Seated on a bench in a clear pool, they grace the residence of the president.

STATELY IMAGE of blindfolded justice (*below*) sits proudly on a stone pedestal in Brasília's Plaza of the Three Powers, the windswept center of the spacious city.

BLOSSOMING from a broad rooftop, two massive concrete bowls house the two chambers of Brazil's Congress. Doorless and windowless, the assembly halls are reached from the building below. A flat lid covers the dishlike deputies' chamber.

TROPICAL PRODUCE is carried to Manaus from tiny outposts along the Rio Negro. The river highways of the Amazon area carry only a small volume of commerce.

5

The Slow
Awakening
of a Giant

IN the Brazilian national anthem there are lines which Brazilians have for years found amusing. They speak of the giant land "eternally lying in a splendid cradle." The lines were true until a very short time ago. But now there are obvious signs that slowly, in spite of great problems and a thousand difficulties, the giant is at last waking up.

While Brazil remains in many ways an agricultural country—agriculture produces almost 30 per cent of the national income and employs more than half of the working population—revenue from industry is beginning to overtake that from agriculture. In 1960 Brazil produced more than 134,000 vehicles with parts made almost entirely within the country. Steel production is increasing, and Brazil is now turning out more than 2 million net tons a year, compared with 350,000 net tons in the immediate postwar period. Even appliances are beginning to be produced in volume.

Remarkable as this achievement is, it does not necessarily mean that Brazil will soon become an industrial colossus. The country has ample resources—its hydroelectric potential alone is the world's greatest: 80 million kilowatts. But Brazilians, it is said, "collect the fruit without planting the tree." They have a national penchant for skimming off quick profits instead of laying the foundation for solid future earnings. The economic history of Brazil could almost be told in its long succession of spectacular booms. Brazil's economy was dominated by sugar, gold and coffee in succession, with brief interludes devoted to other products. But the country is today trying to diversify, rather than depend on single crops or industries.

One of Brazil's earliest occupations was cattle raising, and it was necessarily an imported one. The Portuguese discoverers had been surprised to find that the Indians had no domestic animals, or at least no useful domestic animals. The Indians did keep many pets, referred to by the Portuguese as *bichos de estimação*: dogs, monkeys and birds.

Hence one of the first, and very difficult, undertakings of the Portuguese was to bring to Brazil all the domesticated animals they were accustomed to at home. In the middle of the 16th Century cattle were brought to Bahia from Portugal and the Cape Verde Islands. They were the forebears of the cattle of the plains of the northeast.

Cattle were introduced in the south as early as 1532. The settlers who followed the *bandeirantes* took with them cows, horses, pigs and goats. Later they drove the descendants of these animals through the one natural passage which penetrates the coastal mountain range and into the open stretch west of São Paulo. Horses and cows were allowed to range freely. As in the early days in the west of the United States, rustling and the roundup of wild herds —for the most part strays from the Jesuit villages—were important aspects of the life and legend of the region.

ALTHOUGH from the beginning sugar was the principal product in the northeast, cattle were a stimulus to colonization and the opening of new lands. In search of pastures for their herds, cattlemen pushed deep into the northeastern interior. Cattle raising changed from a simple adjunct of the great plantations to an independent activity. From it came the so-called "leather civilization" that developed in this whole vast region of Brazil during the first centuries of the country's history. The horse, upon which cattle raising depended, today inseparable from the gaucho of the Brazilian pampas and the *vaqueiro* of the northeast, became acclimated throughout the country. Today Brazil has more than 8 million horses.

In the northeast most of the cattle are descendants of the original herds. They are small and give little milk, but are tough and resistant. Over the years, the government and progressive cattle raisers have improved the stock throughout the country by crossing it with the zebu or Brahman, introduced from India. This animal is well-adapted to the harsh northern conditions of heat, drought and meager pasturage, and it thrives where the finest European stock dies off or quickly sickens and degenerates. Zebus, with their high shoulder humps, high-domed skulls and long, drooping ears, have become common in most of Brazil, adding an exotic yet somehow not incongruous note to the landscape.

AT the turn of the 20th Century, zebus were imported into the huge section of fine cattleland in Minas Gerais which is called the "Minas Triangle," and which is now the center of the cattle industry. They became acclimated so successfully that zebu owning became a passion with cattle raisers; prices soared, zebu buying and selling became a form of gambling and there was wild speculation. In the 1920s the fever reached such a pitch that a single good bull brought as much as $7,500, compared to an average price of $250 for bulls of European breed.

Outside the beef-raising Triangle, the cattle of Minas Gerais are dairy cattle, and their products, including the white Minas cheese seen on almost every table at least once a day, are sold everywhere. Beef cattle need huge tracts of land, and with the rapid and progressive industrialization of the central-southern part of the country the cattle are being shifted to the wilder regions of Goiás and the Pantanal in Mato

Grosso, which offer favorable conditions and are also near the biggest consumer of beef, the state of São Paulo.

In Pará, especially on the island of Marajó, the Indian water buffalo has been introduced and seems completely at home. The wilderness and abundant rivers and swamps of the huge island provide the kind of semiaquatic life this semidomesticated beast prefers, while ordinary cattle, even the zebu, do not thrive there. The buffalo present some small problems on occasion, though. Buffalo like to lean on things and meditate. Sometimes they lean on their owners' frail mud-and-wattle houses, which collapse under them.

IN a country with few refrigerators, the industry of making *charque,* a dried, salted meat which does not spoil easily and which is usually cooked with the staple black beans and rice, is very important. The industry started in the northeast and was taken by immigrants to Rio Grande do Sul. Although outranked in total number of cattle by Minas Gerais, this state now raises the country's finest beef and is a center of the meat-packing industry. With 72.8 million head, Brazil is second only to the U.S. in number of beef cattle, but not in beef production, primarily because of poor disease control, inadequate transport and refrigeration facilities, and antiquated methods.

The largest herds of sheep—Brazil has some 22 million head—are also in Rio Grande do Sul, and crude wool is beginning to rank as an important export. With cotton, a major export for years, these herds also provide some material for the textile industry, which has grown enormously in the last decade.

The country's immense coastline and teeming rivers should make fishing and processing fish much more important industries than they are. But commercial exploitation has just begun, and fish still represent one of the greatest undeveloped resources of the country. In the states of Pará and Amazonas there is, for example, the *pirarucu,* the "fresh-water codfish," weighing up to 500 pounds. The *pirarucu* is an important item in the diet of the river people.

The commercial catch in the Amazon runs to only 90,000 tons a year, largely because fishing techniques used in the river are still primitive, as are those of many of the coastal fishermen. The beautiful, traditional *jangadas* of the northeast are merely rafts made of balsa trunks lashed together. They have one sail, and every object aboard must be tied fast to the deck. The fishermen venture on the high seas aboard the *jangadas,* but the hauls of fish they bring back are usually so small that it has been said that the real place for the picturesque *jangada* is in the folklore museum.

Some modernization has been taking place in the fishing industry. Several Japanese firms have formed motorized fleets in the south, specializing in tuna and whale. One large whale-processing plant has been built at Cabo Frio, a coast town east of Rio. Whales are abundant, and whale meat is being urged on a somewhat reluctant public in the coastal markets as the cheapest form of meat. Lobster fishing has also been increasing, chiefly in Pernambuco and Ceará. Canning factories are being built along the coast.

COFFEE has been subject to as many ups and downs as any other Brazilian resource, but it has certainly not been troubled by under-exploitation. For many years it has been Brazil's best-known product; coffee has been the greatest item of export and the biggest source of income. Brazil produced almost 4 billion pounds in 1960. It supplied the world with nearly half its coffee, earning the country 56 per cent of its total foreign-trade income.

Brazilian coffee had modest origins. Early in the 18th Century, a Brazilian stole shoots from French Guiana, where the French had started coffee plantations. The trees were first cultivated in the state of Pará. Later, seeds and shoots were distributed throughout the country. Cultivation remained small-scale until the 19th Century, when coffee had its first great phase in Rio de Janeiro and Minas. The cultivation of coffee in these states, particularly in

Rio de Janeiro, depended directly on slave labor, and coffee profits made the fortunes of the Rio de Janeiro barons. With the abolition of slavery in 1888 the barons went bankrupt.

São Paulo did not have as much slave labor, and was far-sighted enough to encourage immigration. In the crucial years before and after abolition, immigrants—principally from Portugal and Italy—came in great numbers. In addition to this labor supply, São Paulo had its marvelous *terra roxa* (purple earth), which, according to the Paulistas, God created especially for the raising of coffee. Also coffee, which already had been named "the vampire," since within a few years it exhausted the soil, had declined in the state of Rio. In the year of abolition, for example, the states of Rio and Minas produced twice as much coffee as São Paulo; 10 years later São Paulo was producing much more than both states together. Nevertheless, even with improved methods of cultivation, the *terra roxa* of São Paulo in turn began to be exhausted. Coffee continued its march to the south and to the west; in the late 1920s tracts of the precious dark red soil were found in the wild country of northwestern Paraná. Like a green army, the coffee trees of the planters triumphantly took over, pushing back the virgin forest and driving the wild animals farther into the interior. In the shade of the coffee trees new towns were born. A typical example is Londrina, a modern and prosperous city located where only a few decades ago stood the untouched forest. At present the coffee trees are penetrating into the state of Mato Grosso.

AS the mainstay of the Brazilian economy, coffee has suffered various crises, during which the entire national life has been threatened. The appearance of Africa among the coffee producers created one of the most serious of these crises in the 1950s. Although still the coffee leader of the world, Brazil has had to face previously unknown competition, and the competition is constantly becoming more acute. Brazil cannot today sell all its coffee; in 1960 it had an accumulated stockpile of more than 5 billion pounds.

Repeated crises in the coffee market are having the effect of arousing the country to the necessity of agricultural diversification; Brazil is attempting to expand exports of other products like sugar, tobacco and fruit. The coffee problem has also stimulated the growth of industrialization, chiefly in São Paulo, today Brazil's most prosperous state. It has undergone a tremendous boom since World War II. There was no heavy-machinery industry before the war; today there are more than 45 major plants in São Paulo. In 1959 alone, the state manufactured more than 15,000 machine tools. It produces 53 per cent of the country's paper, 54 per cent of its textiles and 58 per cent of its chemicals, and it is a major bulwark of the foreign market, exporting more than 1.6 million tons of manufactured goods a year. With the nearby state of Guanabara, São Paulo contributes almost half of Brazil's domestic income.

AT the center of this industrial complex lies the city of São Paulo itself. It was a quiet town of 25,000 people only 80 years ago. Today it covers 535 square miles and, with a population of 4.8 million, is the eighth largest metropolis in the world. Its traffic problem is even worse than that of New York, and it has a bustling, cosmopolitan atmosphere, although with its white, modern skyscrapers and many parks it remains intensely Brazilian.

Unlike the prosperous south, the states of the northeast remain almost wholly agricultural. There sugar, which had its earlier heyday of monoculture before being dethroned by coffee, is still the basis of the economy—although cotton and cacao are grown in large quantities. Sugar developed even as Brazil itself developed; it could almost be said that the first Portuguese arrived with shoots of sugar cane under their arms. The rich northeastern sugar plantations of Pernambuco and Bahia were major factors in luring the Dutch to invade in the 17th Century. Most of the profitable sugar growing is now done in the south, but in

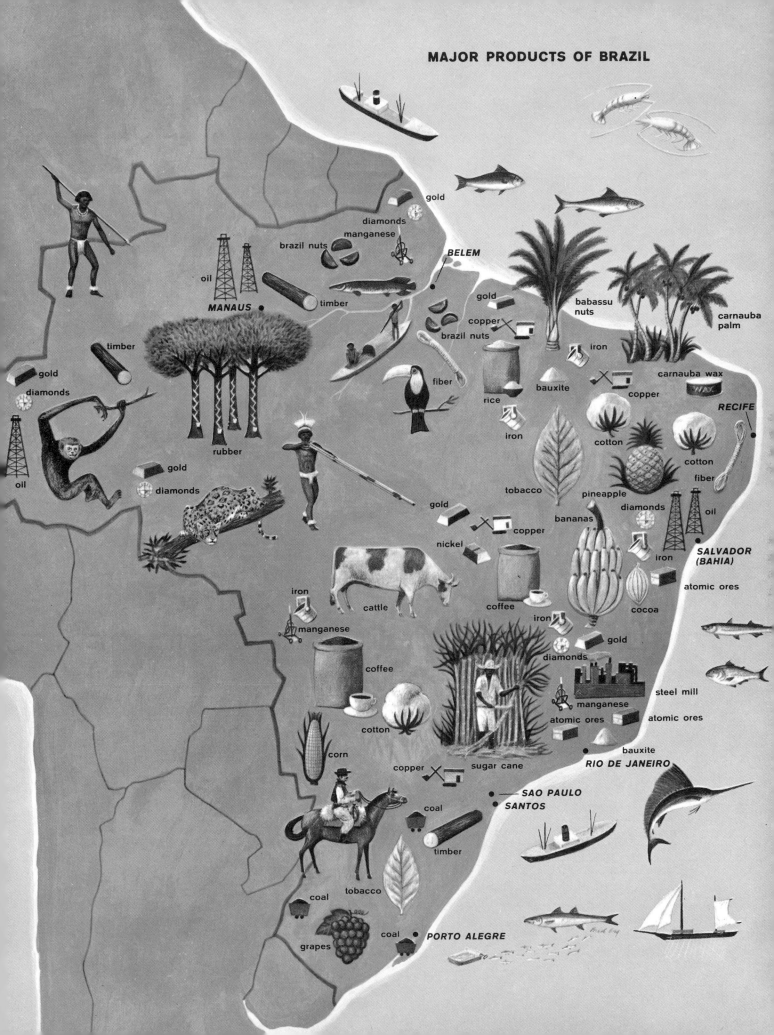

MAJOR PRODUCTS OF BRAZIL

Pernambuco, Alagôas and Paraíba, the cane fields still stretch to the horizon. Great refineries, which are beginning to take the place of the primitive old ones, are improving the product. But the methods of cultivation are extremely primitive, almost semifeudal; and the sugar workers are among the poorest and most long-suffering of Brazilian peoples. There is today a strong movement among enlightened Brazilians for reform of the agrarian situation throughout the northeast. It is indeed a highly explosive area, ripe for Communist exploitation.

One product of the sugar cane is *aguardente,* generally called *cachaça* or *pinga.* A clear, fiery, powerful drink made since colonial times, it is known as "the brandy of the poor." *Cachaça* is now being exported. There is no Brazilian product surrounded by so much folklore as *cachaça;* a whole cycle of songs celebrates it. The names by which it is called, mostly affectionate nicknames—"the grandmother," "the little blonde," "the thread of gold"—show the esteem in which *cachaça* is regarded. When a man takes a drink at the nearest corner bar, he always spits out a little of the first mouthful onto the floor, as an offering to whichever saint he believes to be the donor of the liquor.

R UBBER, too, once played a major economic role. The source of great but brief wealth, Amazon rubber suffered a blow in 1910 when the plantations in Malaya and the Dutch East Indies began to outproduce and undersell it in the world market. The towns that had flourished in the valley of the Amazon were rapidly transformed into dead or dying communities. The city of Manaus, situated near the meeting point of the Amazon and the Rio Negro, was the rubber capital of the world until the collapse of the market. Rich and luxurious, with a huge opera house, it imported troops of singers and dancers. Large ships made it a regular port of call. To the east of Manaus, Henry Ford established experimental plantations, Fordlândia and Belterra, in the late 1920s and early 1930s, but, finding the project unprofitable, abandoned it. Today owned by the

government, the project still produces a small amount of rubber.

During World War II, when Japan seized the plantations of Malaya and the Dutch East Indies, there was a brief resuscitation in Amazonian rubber. But Brazil today imports some $40 million worth of Asian rubber each year. The Amazon, deprived of the market for its principal wealth, has also been attempting diversification in recent years. The area now produces substantial quantities of Brazil nuts, jute, lumber, sugar cane and vegetable oils as well as manganese.

L IKE other Brazilian resources, lumber has had its brief fling, but it too has yet to reach its potential. In the Amazon basin alone, there are at least 5 trillion cubic feet of timber, and there are vast forests of prime woods in the south. One of the most attractive features of the national landscape is commonest in the states of Paraná and Santa Catarina—the groves of araucarias, the Brazilian pine tree. They are beautiful, very tall trees with straight trunks and arched, bare branches terminating in characteristic cup-shaped bunches of needles. Besides being beautiful, the araucaria is extremely useful; its wood constitutes the principal wealth of the region in which it grows. So sought after was this wood that the government was forced to pass a law in 1942 prohibiting excessive cutting and providing for replanting.

With more than 600 known varieties, Brazil has more palm trees than any country in the world. They are rich sources of fiber, oils and fuel. From the leaves of the carnauba, an elegant, tall palm that flourishes only in northeast Brazil, comes a sticky deposit rather like beeswax which, when gathered, powdered and melted by a difficult and primitive process, produces the famous carnauba wax. It is used in the manufacture of phonograph records, polishes and varnishes. The carnauba is one of the principal economic supports of the states of Ceará, Piauí and Maranhão, and the people of the dry *sertões* say that is the compensation given them by God for the scourge of drought

—since when the weather turns wet the palm produces no wax.

Tobacco is raised in most of Brazil, and has been for centuries. It was important trade merchandise for the slave dealers. It has developed into an industry in Bahia, whose cigars are famous and good enough to be compared with those of Cuba. Bahia cigarettes are also widely distributed, but the greatest number of cigarette factories is in the state of Rio Grande do Sul.

The European grape, introduced by Italian immigrants, grows very well in Rio Grande do Sul. The wine industry has developed rapidly and today Brazilians are proud of some of their wines, champagnes and cognacs. In 1960 nearly 8 million gallons were exported to France. Also important to Rio Grande do Sul is wheat, although far from enough is produced to make Brazil self-sufficient. The country usually manages to produce enough corn, beans and rice for domestic consumption.

Only recently has there been much interest in making use of Brazilian fruit for exportation or canning. Oranges are now exported on a large scale. Bananas, of which Brazil is the world's largest grower, are principally grown in São Paulo. The cashew fruit of the northeast provides the valuable cashew nut; the fruit is also processed in the form of syrups and pastes. And then there is the guava. Guava paste, accompanied by white cheese, is the favorite dessert all over Brazil.

BRAZIL'S greatest mineral resource is iron. There are practically inexhaustible veins in the country, located mainly in the state of Minas. It is estimated that there are 65 billion tons of iron ore in Brazil, 35 per cent of the world's total reserve. The lack of high-quality coking coal has until recently prevented the development of steel mills commensurate in number with the quantity of ore. However, the coal of Santa Catarina, although of an inferior quality, has been energetically exploited, and the result has been the great steel mills of Volta Redonda, whose construction began in 1942 with U.S. aid. Brazil's iron and steel industry is now the largest industry in Latin America, and exploitation of the ore has barely begun.

The same is true of other mineral reserves. There are deposits of just about every known mineral, including precious and semiprecious stones, scattered throughout the country, some in vast quantities. Only with denser population in these areas and more specialized techniques will Brazil be able to profit from these hidden riches. In Espírito Santo and other areas the government is at present exploring layers of monazite sands rich in radioactive ores.

A MATTER of considerable controversy in Brazil is the extent of petroleum reserves. Some geologists have suggested that the vast sedimentary basins of the Amazon and Paraná, encompassing nearly 2 million square miles, contain extensive reserves. But so far only traces of oil have been found. Due to a fear of foreign exploitation, oil exploration and production were restricted in 1953 to a single government monopoly, Petrobrás. Despite valiant wildcatting at a cost of some $50 million a year, Brazil produces only some 30 per cent of its own crude requirements, most of it from the wells in Bahia. And even if there are extensive reserves in the upper Amazon valley, geologists believe that they lie under rock and would present difficult and expensive problems. Transport would not be a problem, because of the nearness of the navigable Amazon. Throughout most of the country, however, transport is one of the basic problems which Brazil must solve before it can begin real exploitation of its truly magnificent resources. Today, Brazil has nearly 24,000 miles of railroads, but most of them are short-haul, east-west lines which penetrate inland only a short distance from the coast. Many of them are of different gauges, and there are few north-south connections in any event. The highway network still under construction will of course help to solve this problem. Indeed, the giant is awakening, but before he can exercise his strength he will have to take steps that Brazilians wish had been made long years ago.

An Expansion Fueled by Coffee Riches

For almost 150 years coffee has been the economic colossus of Brazil. Nearly half the world's coffee comes from Brazilian trees and most of the nation's vital foreign revenue comes from coffee exports. Though the world coffee market is beset by fluctuating prices, coffee remains the pivotal Brazilian asset: the collapse of the coffee market in 1929 helped bring down the first republic a year later. Even São Paulo's industrial expansion has depended on capital derived from the surrounding coffee plantations. But the coffee revenues now financing the new roads, dams and mining operations may eventually free Brazil from the dominance of coffee.

COFFEE WORKERS rake berries (*left*) so that they will all dry thoroughly. Coffee beans are the seeds of the berry.

COFFEE TREES set in trim rows on a plantation in Paraná (*opposite*) each yield about a pound of coffee yearly.

KEY MINERAL RESOURCES provide a solid basis for a growing heavy industry

SHAVED MOUNTAIN, 210 miles north of Rio, is made up almost completely of high-grade iron ore. Since mining operations began, the mountain has been reduced by more than 400 feet. Tremendous iron deposits like this and a supply of vital manganese have enabled Brazil to build the largest steel industry in Latin America.

COSMOPOLITAN SKYLINE of São Paulo testifies to the city's spectacular boom. Today 3.7 million people and 23,000 factories are housed in the hard-driving city.

INDUSTRIAL SCION, Francisco ("Cicillo") Matarazzo (*opposite*) is São Paulo's leading art patron. He and his family own Latin America's largest business empire.

At the famed Carnival in Rio, a dance group struts with canes before a crowded grandstand. Despite its size and elaborateness, the

celebration manages to retain much of its original spontaneity.

6

Graceful and Popular Skills

POPULAR arts and handicrafts are still flourishing in rural Brazil as they have not in the United States since colonial days. More sophisticated art, of course, comes from the cities. From the cities, too, come the manufactured products, good and bad, artistic or trashy, that contemporary man buys to satisfy his esthetic cravings, instead of making things for himself as he used to do. But the poor people of Brazil, the rural people of the coast or the interior, have almost no cash income and can buy almost nothing. They still make many of the things they wear or use, and these articles are often of very high artistic value.

Since the poor man also has no entertainment (or had not until the advent of the radio) he produces his own: songs, ballads, dances and traditional, sometimes elaborate folk plays, which appear according to the saints' days and the seasons. He weaves cotton, plaits straw and cane, makes pottery, and carves wood and stone. The richness and variety of these native arts owe much to the fact that, like the Brazilian people themselves, they are culturally mixed: they were inherited from the Portuguese and Moors and influenced by the Indians and by African slaves. Occasionally now, in the southern part of the country, influences of German, Italian, Japanese and Polish immigrants can be noticed as well.

A GOOD example of this intermingling is that in Brazilian folk pottery the potter's wheel is not used, although it was familiar to the Portuguese for centuries before they came to Brazil. This is almost certainly because the present-day folk potters derived their art from Indian rather than from Portuguese tradition. Even without the wheel, for a thousand years and more, the Indians have made magnificent bowls and urns, sometimes of enormous size: huge pots for fermenting liquor, and funerary urns big enough to hold the body of an adult sitting in fetal position. These pots are built up by "coiling," a technique by which the potter winds long thin ropes of clay round and round until the desired height and shape are reached. The Brazilian folk potters make smaller pots of great elegance in this primitive way, decorating them in black, white and earth colors, and polishing them with the rinds of fruit.

All pots intended for practical use are made by women (a convention taken from the Indians), but men often make clay statuettes. Painted and glazed, or in the original clay color, these figures depict the types and activities of rural society: cowboys, soldiers, priests and hunters; weddings, funerals and jaguar hunts. Women make toys and, occasionally, figures too. In one town in the state of Ceará, particularly, the women make miniature pots and dishes, furniture and toy animals, often surprisingly like the Greek and Roman toys that survive in museums. Manufactured articles, highly prized but too expensive to buy, are often copied in clay—pots for babies, lamps, washboards, even realistic clocks and watches.

In the northeastern cattle-raising regions leatherworking techniques have been highly developed. Cowhide and goatskin are the usual materials, although deerskin, being softer, is the most valuable. The cowboy's leather clothes are made to protect him from the spiny trees and low-growing cacti of the area. His costume is very much like medieval armor made in leather: leggings, serving the same purpose as an American cowboy's chaps, but tight-fitting and extending down over the top of the foot; an apron; a chest-protector; and over all, a leather doublet with long sleeves overlapped by leather gloves. On his head he wears a leather hat, with a leather cockade. These garments are often fancifully decorated: stamped, embroidered or inlaid in different-colored leathers.

B ESIDES the art of pottery, the women of the north and northeast have inherited from their Indian forebears the art of working in straw. In the state of Ceará they weave baskets, fish traps, coarse and fine sieves and mats to be used as ceilings below the naked rafters of their homes. In the state of Pará, cane furniture is made at home for commercial sale. Travelers on the Amazon are sometimes startled to see a large wicker rocking chair approaching them across the water, balanced on the bow of an almost invisible canoe—although the traveler at that point hardly would seem to be a likely purchaser of a rocking chair or a baby's high chair or a settee. One of the most beautiful and characteristic arts of the same region is the weaving of hammocks with thread made from palm leaves. These hammocks are soft and supple, straw-colored, with black designs. They are not used for sleeping in the night, but are hung on the shady porches for show, for lounging or for conversational siestas. The sleeping hammocks are of cotton, and are either bright plaid or all white—the more valuable variety. In the *casa grande*, or big house, of a ranch or plantation, the number of hammock chests, in which dozens of snow-white hammocks are packed away with sweet-smelling herbs, used to be an indication of the owner's wealth. One *casa grande* in the state of Ceará kept 120 hammocks in its chests for the use of guests, and in addition there were special priests' hammocks, whose lace borders displayed crosses, crossed lances and other symbols of the Roman Catholic faith. This ranch was established in 1850 and was named, half jokingly and half hopefully, "The California," because of the stories that had reached Brazil of the gold discovered in California by the forty-niners. It still bears the name.

Another tradition inherited from the Indian is the decoration of gourds called *cúias*, which are used for drinking and for bathing. They are always enameled black, and the formula of the enamel is a secret, handed down from generation to generation. After the enameling, the decorations are incised into the gourd. They are either left in the natural gourd color or brightly painted. They show such subjects as flowers or fruits or flags, and such sentiments as *Souvenir, Mother Love, Happy Birthday* or the historical slogan *Independence or Death!*

From the Portuguese the Brazilian women inherited the art of lacemaking, exquisitely fine work that taxes the eyes and the patience. A hand's-breadth often takes more than a day to do. Lace made from thread of banana-leaf fibers instead of commercial thread is particularly rare and valuable. Crocheted or knitted lace and embroideries are also very beautiful when the old patterns have not been forgotten or vulgarized. There is a group of folk songs devoted to lacemaking; some of them relate the saga of a notorious bandit of the northeast, Lampião, who was shot in 1938. Strange to say, the riding song of Lampião's followers was "The Lacemaker": "Oh, lacemaker! / Teach me to make lace / And I'll teach you how to love...."

IN the gold-mining regions of Minas Gerais, Goiás and Bahia, the goldsmith's art was early developed. The stones set in these old pieces are rough diamonds or some of the many Brazilian semiprecious stones: aquamarines, topazes, amethysts and tourmalines. A great deal of work is still done in Bahia with gold and silver, ivory and coral, often in the form of lucky charms, especially the *figa*, or "fig." This immemorial image of a clenched fist with the thumb protruding between the first two fingers is seen everywhere in Brazil. Small *figas* are hung around babies' necks, along with a holy medal. Larger wooden ones are hung on the walls. Also from Bahia are the *balangandãs*, jingling bunches of charms formerly worn by slave women at their waists, and now very valuable. The charms, several inches long, include pomegranates, cashew fruits, musical instruments, phallic symbols and objects used in the rites of the cult of *macumba*. Other articles relating to this cult are produced in Bahia, including devils in iron and the magnificently embroidered silk banners used in the processions of the "churches."

MACUMBA, usually called *candomblé* in Bahia, its chief center, is a highly developed religion, resembling the voodoo religion of the Caribbean. Originating in the African cults brought to Brazil by the slaves, it mixes black and white gods, goddesses and saints in a fantastic half-pagan, half-Christian pantheon. St. George owes part of his popularity in Brazil to the fact that he has been made into a *macumba* saint, and there are many such transformations.

In *macumba* rituals, cocks and other animals are sacrificed, hypnotic states are induced by music and singing, and members of the church become "possessed" by a particular god, acquiring his attributes and speaking for him. Black magic as well as white or "good" magic is practiced. Frequently at night, on country roads, along beaches or in city doorways, candles can be seen glimmering. A black candle, cigars and a black bottle of *cachaça*, or a white candle, white flowers, a chicken and a clear bottle of *cachaça*—these are *macumba* hexes or offerings, witnesses to the superstitious devotion of millions of Brazilians to this cult.

In other sections of the northeast, land of bandits as well as religious fanatics, the local workmen specialize in silver-mounted knives with flattened handles, to be worn in high boots, and daggers with handles of enamel, ivory or gold filigree. So cheerfully bellicose is this region even now that during a friendly *futebol* game between the teams of two rival towns, above the applause and vendors' cries of "Popcorn!" and "Orange Croosh!" one can hear the voice of a man hawking the locally made knives from a basket on his back: "Get your little daggers for after the game!"

The art of the saint makers is traditional in the northeast. Not many years ago almost every little rural household chapel had its wooden images carved by the local saint maker. In the 18th Century, the bodies of the saints were sometimes hollowed out, in order to hide gold or diamonds from the government inspectors, and the expression "a hollow saint" is still used to mean a hypocritical person. In some areas, saints are still being carved. For the last 20 years, however, the priests, not appreciating the primitive in art and needing money for their churches, have been selling or exchanging these often very remarkable wood carvings for sentimental contemporary statues of tinted plaster. Sad to say, the taste of their rural congregations has deteriorated as well, so that they now prefer these mass-produced statues to the old, original works.

BECAUSE of this, many of the saint makers have turned instead to making "miracles" —that is, representations of parts of the body ostensibly cured of disease by the miraculous intervention of a saint and presented in gratitude at that saint's shrine. Each of the most popular shrines around the country has rooms full of these objects, so that the shrines are veritable museums of popular art. Legs, arms, heads, ears and eyes, as well as hearts and other inner organs of wood or wax, attest miraculous cures. There may also be beautiful or, at least, quaint statues of miraculously cured domestic animals—horses, cows, goats and poultry. And along with them are paintings of other miracles: fishing boats saved from storms, hunters from wild beasts or deadly snakes, and souls from swarms of pursuing devils.

In the field of popular sculpture, however, undoubtedly the greatest achievement is the creation of the figureheads used on boats on the Rio São Francisco. Called *carrancas,* the figureheads depict animals, women and characters from Afro-Brazilian folklore, but one of the favorites is always the "Great Worm," the most dreadful of the spirits that live in the river. Some of these figureheads are very fine, towering several feet above the bow of the boat and carved in a strong and simple style reminiscent of Romanesque sculpture. Unfortunately, *carrancas* are being used less and less today, and the art of carving them is dying out.

Brazilians of the *sertão,* or backlands, prize their folk poets, whom they call "singers." These men lead the lives of wanderers; their verses, sung to their own accompaniment on violins or guitars, are improvisations, but in strict and very ancient forms and meters. They appear at rural *festas* and engage in duels of verse that sometimes go on for 24 hours, with the singers stopping only to drink and eat. The contestants try to outlast each other in ideas, rhymes and good humor. The loser is the one whose rhymes finally fail him.

The singers are privileged people in these little communities. They also have a high opinion of themselves and of their "memories," their word for poetic talent. As one of them boasts, "There's no man like the King / No woman like the Queen / No saint like God Almighty / And no memory like mine. . . ."

BEFORE the advent of the radio, the singers were the newspapers of the backlands; even today they continue to produce prompt and dramatic verse accounts of all the more sensational news. A few days after President Getúlio Vargas' suicide in 1954, a "Brazilian Writer" (as he signed himself) of Recife produced a ballad-pamphlet called "Getúlio in Heaven," which still sells in the outdoor markets. The 1961 flight of Yuri Gagarin, the Soviet cosmonaut, was put into verse almost immediately after the event, as was the resignation of President Jânio Quadros. Usually the singers (who cannot write—someone else takes down their verses for them) sing their compositions and then sell them in pamphlet form to bystanders.

The drama is still another folk art very much alive in Brazil. Christmas, the New Year and many saints' days are celebrated everywhere with *festas* in the form of plays or dances that vary according to local tradition and the racial group predominating in the region. In the north and northeast the favorite celebration is the *Bumba-meu-boi* (Beat My Ox). As in the classical and Elizabethan theater, women do not act in the *Bumba-meu-boi*. A little group of men acts out a story about an ox who dances, sings, grows sick, dies and then returns to life amid general rejoicing and additional songs and dances. The stylized figure of the ox, with one or two dancers inside, is followed by other types: the cowboy, the horse, the donkey, the doctor, the priest (who comes to give the last rites to the dying ox) and clowns. The action is interspersed with songs and there is always a great deal of ad libbing.

In the coastal regions, the country people execute dances based on the old Portuguese *fandangos* and *cheganças*. In a model ship built on the site of the *festa*, they present the dramatic story of the vessel *Catarineta*, based on an old Portuguese tale in verse that dates from the 17th Century. Where Negroes predominate, the dance is often a "Congo." At the court of King Congo, rivals betray the kingdom to white invaders. The crown prince discovers the plot and is killed; then follows a battle. The characters are richly dressed in velvet capes, satin breeches and golden crowns. The ambassador of the whites is always an imposing Negro dressed like an English admiral, wearing a plumed hat. Perhaps he is Lord Nelson, for the story confuses African, Portuguese and British history impartially.

At Christmastime in many parts of Brazil, the Play of the Shepherds appears. It depicts the shepherds in search of the Christ Child, singing and dancing in His honor. The words, songs and jokes of these primitive plays are traditional, handed down from father to son.

But all the plays and festivals—and there are many more, including a variety of rodeo—pale beside the great, annual, three-day Brazilian frenzy of song and dance, Carnival. This world-famous institution, which takes place throughout the country, reached Brazil by way of the old Portuguese Shrove Tuesday celebrations. The Brazilian version originally was a simple affair, and most of the rough fun consisted in throwing basins of cold water and sacks of flour. In the cities and towns of Brazil, the one-day celebration was gradually transformed into the huge affair it is today —a mass masquerade, an enormous public ball with dancing in the streets and organized parades of dancers as well. In Rio hundreds of private balls are given at the same time. The paraders belong to groups from different town districts, each group wearing its elaborate—and often costly—special costume. The festivities go on all night for the three nights preceding Ash Wednesday and all ordinary business comes to a complete stop. The sambas of the year are constantly in the air; the streets are filled with slowly moving samba-ing crowds. The air is thick with confetti and streamers and the odor of the "perfume shooters"—flasks of scented ether that shoot a fine spray, not only perfuming the air but giving the person who gets hit a momentary pin-point shock of icy cold. Women

SONG OF THE INTERIOR

Se eu não beber fico seco
Seco não posso cantar.
E não cantando estou morto
E morto não posso amar.
Não amando fico louco,
E louco vão me amarrar . . .

If I don't drink I get dry
And dry I cannot sing.
If I do not sing I die
And dead I cannot love.
I go mad if I can't love,
And if I'm mad, they'll cart me off . . .

BACKLANDS VERSE, composed by illiterate "singers," is a major form of entertainment in rural areas. Love and romance are favorite topics.

samba, babies solemnly rising and falling rhythmically in their arms. The crowd is happy and good-humored.

Carnival is one of the greatest folk spectacles left on earth. Or perhaps one should say that it was, because in the big cities, at least, Carnival unfortunately is rapidly being spoiled. Commercialism and a false idea of what appeals to the tourist are partly to blame. Hollywood has had its dire effect, too. For example, a few years ago Carnival seemed to have turned into a movie nightmare. A Biblical epic had recently been popular, and thousands of Davids and Bathshebas samba-ed in the streets in monotonous and unoriginal getups.

MUCH of the fun at Carnival has also been spoiled by the government's forbidding costumes or floats that make sport of politicians, the Church or the military. Some of the cleverest displays of wit were formerly inspired by these old reliable objects of satire.

But radio and loudspeakers have done the most damage. The virtue of Carnival has always been its spontaneity and the fact that all the songs, music and dances came directly from the people themselves. When commercial songwriters start composing songs for it, and when these songs are broadcast long before Carnival, all charm is lost. Also, when thousands of participants, samba-ing along and singing the year's favorite in unison, are confronted with a loudspeaker blaring the same samba or another one in a different tempo, all singing and dancing naturally stop, and the people shuffle along like sheep. Advertising over the loudspeaker interrupts the dances, too. Photographers have also been allowed to interfere with the street dancers, breaking into even the prize-winning performances to get good shots. In Rio during the past two Carnivals the spectators finally whistled and booed particularly obnoxious photographers off the streets.

In smaller cities, however, the festival still has its authentic folklore flavor. The ordinary man goes out to play, or "to break," as he calls having fun. If he can afford it, he dresses as a prince, a rooster, an Indian, the devil, or the always popular skeleton. Or he goes dressed as a woman, as thousands do. The more modest Carnival-goer can improvise a primitive costume simply by stitching a cape with leaves, which is supposed to make him look like an Indian. Or he can shave a strip of hair down the crown of his head, paint it red and appear with a tomahawk sticking in his skull. He may even shave his head completely, painting it blue or green. With an umbrella he sets out to dance the *frêvo,* a wild and acrobatic number which is performed half-crouching. If all else fails, he can go in rags, simply as a "dirty one."

Rio de Janeiro has an original institution, the samba schools, most of which luckily have not been spoiled by commercialism. These are not exactly schools, but are more like clubs, whose members (almost entirely poor Negroes from the *favelas*) meet throughout the year to learn the songs and dances for the coming Carnival. Much time and money are devoted to these schools. The songs are real folk music. The themes are love (most important) or social criticism: the government, the cost of living and politics. A general theme is given the schools for each Carnival, such as "Rio in the Time of the Viceroys" or "The Discovery of Gold." In carrying out the "gold" theme, the women members of one school danced with huge imitation gold nuggets sparkling on top of their heads.

A FAVORITE costume year after year seems vaguely patterned on the costumes worn in the time of Louis XV. Where else in the world could one see a hundred male Negroes, in blue and white and silver Louis XV costumes seeded with tiny white light bulbs, and wearing white curled wigs and plumed hats, dancing down the middle of the main street at 4 a.m.? After them come the women, wearing wonderful headdresses, dressed in satins glinting with the same lights, hung with ropes of silver and blue glass beads, and singing as they dance—courtly, ravishing and gracious, swaying to incessant, hypnotic but not fast music—a fairyland for a night.

Patchily dressed, Rio neighbors turn out for impromptu Carnival merrymaking. The frenzy is usually good-humored and sober.

The Vivid Folkways of an Urbane City

Despite the inroads of cash, commerce and the movies, the popular arts have not yet vanished from Brazilian cities as they have from cities elsewhere. In cosmopolitan Rio, the Carnival still draws on the skills of amateur dance clubs and local samba writers. Rio's folk spirit also survives in other forms. The *macumba* cult, which blends African and Christian beliefs and rituals, is a highly obsessional worship evolved by poor Negroes to fill their spiritual needs.

BEMUSED CELEBRANTS, a chubby ballerina and a mustached potentate are among the few in Rio who remain stationary amid the musical gyrations of the Carnival.

CARNIVAL BELLE flossily dressed in her samba costume (*opposite*) belongs to one of the many Rio "samba schools" which compete for prizes during the festival.

FOLK COMEDY cherished for centuries in the small towns of the hinterland combines songs, dance and ribald humor to bring welcome mirth to rural areas

HELPFUL CLOWNS are part of a group gathered to revive a cowboy's dead ox in the folk play *Bumba-meu-boi*, or "Beat My Ox," which is enacted at festival time.

EMBROIDERED OX manned by a dancer is the hero of the play, which presents cowboys and Indians favorably and shows the farmer as a ludicrous backwoodsman.

INDIAN WARRIOR in the play is represented by an actor in a towering feathered headdress. He helps capture the foolish farmer who has slain the cowboy's beloved ox.

MAGICAL CULTS thrive among the poor in the form of

macumba rites, which are used to summon supernatural spirits

HALF-PAGAN DEVOTEE of *macumba* offers up prayers to Christian statues which are believed to possess extraordinary powers.

PROSTRATE WOMAN, thought to be possessed by a spirit (*right*), lies in a trance induced by the beat of *macumba* drums.

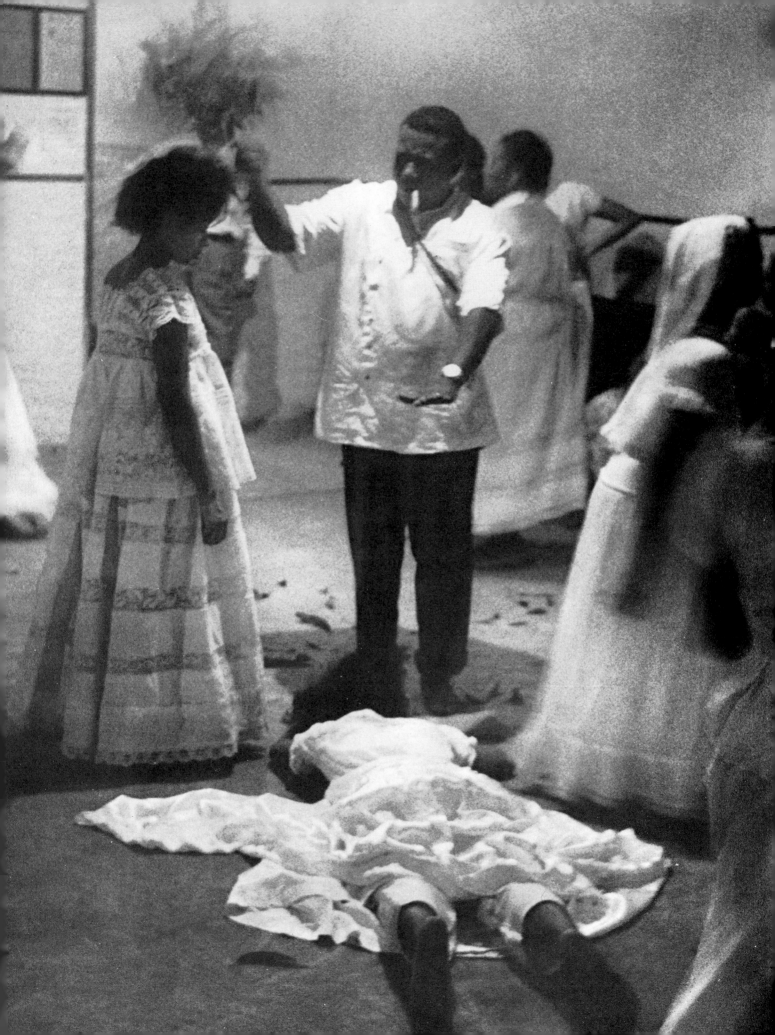

FERVENT PROPHETS were carved in the early 19th Century by Aleijadinho, Brazil's finest sculptor, who created his unique masterpieces in the towns of Minas Gerais.

7

A Merited Respect for the Arts

FEW countries show greater respect for the arts and for culture than Brazil—and in few countries is the respect more merited. For example, there is certainly more good contemporary architecture in Brazil today than in any other of the world's under-industrialized countries. None of the cities along the coast, from Recife to Pôrto Alegre, is without its small but ever-growing cluster of modern "skyscrapers." A Brazilian skyscraper is not necessarily very high, but a 10- or 12-story building thrusts so far above earlier, lower buildings that it qualifies for the title. And each city also has apartment houses, private houses, housing projects,

hospitals and schools, all built in the contemporary idiom. Though as elsewhere the majority may eventually rank only as mediocre attempts to be in style, many are excellent and well-known among architects the world over.

This extraordinary artistic achievement, Brazil's greatest, is due almost entirely to a group of imaginative, energetic, sophisticated and daring architects, most of them still quite young. But Brazilians in general—educated ones, that is—are remarkably architecture-conscious. Everyone seems to have strong opinions about modern architecture, and to be able to speak with assurance of *brise-soleils* ("sun-breakers") or *pilotis* (the pillars raising a building off the ground), which are two of the outstanding features of modern Brazilian building.

Brazil is also one of the few countries where contemporary architecture is encouraged—even favored—by the government. While the United States, for example, was sticking safely to the Greco-Roman for the new Supreme Court building in Washington in the 1930s, Brazil was inaugurating its architectural revolution with the construction of the Ministry of Education and Health in Rio de Janeiro, still considered one of the best examples of contemporary design in the world.

THE young architects who collaborated to produce this building benefited tremendously from the help and advice given them by the French designer Le Corbusier, who was then visiting Brazil. Today they still dominate Brazilian architecture. The group included Oscar Niemeyer and Lúcio Costa, who recently worked on Brasília (see Chapter 4). Another was Jorge M. Moreira, who is known today for his delicate sense of proportion, his refinement of detail and his careful attention to finish—which unfortunately cannot be said of all Brazilian work. Moreira is the architect of the huge University City going up on the outskirts of Rio, which has been long delayed for lack of government funds. The few completed buildings are admirable, and this enormous work will undoubtedly be one of the masterpieces of 20th Century architecture. Affonso Eduardo Reidy, another member of the Ministry of Education team, has always been interested in the sociological side of architecture; among his designs is the large low-cost housing development of Pedregulho, with its own school and playgrounds fitted to the contours of a hill in the suburbs of Rio. Reidy is also the architect of Rio's new Museum of Modern Art. An architect who has become famous in the last decade is Sergio Bernardes, who has perhaps the most playful imagination. His style changes from building to building; he loves the spectacular, and at their best his buildings have an unmistakable gaiety and bravura. His Brazilian pavilion for the 1958 Brussels World's Fair won the exhibit's grand prize for architecture.

There are, of course, others; and all the better-known architects have apprentices—young men from Europe, the United States and Japan, and even an architect from Communist China. As a group the architects seem to be the freest, happiest and least provincial people in the country. They never lack for commissions, and in spite of all the ups and downs of government and real estate, their work flourishes.

The healthy state of architecture is all the more surprising in view of the disadvantages under which the architects are forced to labor. The backwardness of Brazil's steel industry, for example, has long prevented the use of steel-girder construction; almost all of the highest buildings are of reinforced concrete. Until recently few parts were standardized and construction was in consequence expensive and slow. In addition, some parts—such as roofing materials—still suffer from unevenness of quality or impermanence of finish and color. What one famous architectural critic called Brazil's "incredible negligence in the maintenance of public buildings" is, in reality, a combination of this lack of durability of materials plus a lack of government money for upkeep, rather than indifference to appearance.

CONSTRUCTION in Brazil does have other advantages that foreigners are not likely to realize and that may partly account for the country's fine, centuries-old tradition of solid, beautiful buildings. Construction is simplified in many ways: there are no earthquakes or hurricanes to be taken into account, and there need be no heating, screens or heavy insulation. Many houses in the old days had no glass in their windows, just shutters to be barred at night. And though the tropics are popularly thought of as constantly swarming with insects, it is possible, in most of Brazil, to sit in the evenings the year round with open windows. Wandering fireflies or seasonal swarms of moths or termites bother no one, and a burning spiral joss stick helps keep away mosquitoes.

The architect in this semitropical country is spared the impedimenta of cellars, complicated window frames and heating systems. He also has a much freer building code and can put up buildings that in other countries would be considered too experimental or not be allowed because of restrictive zoning laws. On the other hand, wild real-estate speculation hampers him, particularly in the cities, where building lots are too expensive to allow even the wealthy to have yards, and houses are crowded together, cutting off each other's views and breezes.

Copacabana, the world-famous development along one of Rio de Janeiro's beaches, is the outstanding example of this unrestricted land speculation. A solid screen of apartment houses now cuts off every breath of air from the ocean so that only the privileged few along the front can keep cool; the rest of the huge suburb, really a city in itself, swelters between the wall of buildings on one side and the mountains on the other. Furthermore, similar disastrous patterns are being repeated in other parts of Brazil.

AMID all this misuse of the country's natural assets, a force for the good is represented by the noted landscape gardener and botanist Roberto Burle Marx. Like too many Brazilian specialists, Burle Marx is better known outside his own country than in it; many people the world over consider him the greatest landscape gardener today. Until Burle Marx began his work, the average public or large private garden in the tropics or subtropics was an inappropriate, sun-yellowed imitation of the Tuileries, the large formal park in the center of Paris. Burle Marx has altered this by introducing a wealth of native plants and trees in all their exotic colors, shapes and textures, with pools, cascades or falling sheets of water, and with real rocks instead of insipid or melodramatic statuary. For Caracas in Venezuela, he is creating a public garden; he is also working on a big urban redevelopment project in Rio.

Burle Marx has also taken inspiration from the famous mosaic sidewalks of Copacabana Beach, which are laid out in black and white waves parallel to the real waves. This pattern was adapted from the mosaics of Lisbon, which were laid after the great earthquake of 1755 and its subsequent tidal wave. In one new garden, Burle Marx has repeated the pattern in lighter and darker grasses, a beautiful way of using one of the world's simplest decorative materials.

INDEED, Brazilians in general seem to have an instinct for creating beauty out of the humblest of materials. Mud-and-twig houses with their thatches of straw or grass, little stores and bars with their whitewash or pink- or blue-wash walls and their heavy shutters and half doors—all have a highly pleasing effect. Along the Amazon the houses are more likely to be woven of palm leaves, Indian-style, so that they resemble beautiful basketwork. Even the hillside *favelas* of Rio and other cities have a delicate if melancholy beauty. Built of old boards, tin cans, bamboo, sacks or any other material at hand, they are light and graceful, piled up against the slopes like birds' nests, painted in faded colors and festooned with steps, ladders, potted plants and bird cages.

The big old *fazenda* houses, which began to be constructed in the late 16th Century, are generally very handsome. Local adaptations of the farmhouses of Portugal, they have simple floor plans: the high-ceilinged rooms open one into another and there are interior *alcovas,* or bedrooms, where the young daughters of the family led their dreary lives. There is also a chapel and frequently a bedroom and sacristy for a resident padre. And there are always rooms for guests, perhaps with the lock on the outside —for although hospitality was obligatory, it was just as well to be cautious. The early town houses are the same, only narrower and higher. Their sober lines, stone trim and long sloping roofs give them an air of solidity, comfort and elegance. The characteristic concavity of the roofs is derived from buildings observed by the Portuguese in China and Japan.

The use of stone for building came from Portugal, which had long been a stone-building country. The churches of the early arrivals in Brazil were like the houses, and at first carved stone was imported for the façades of both; later good native stonecutters appeared. The smallest, earliest churches had paved squares or roofed porches in front for occasions when there were too many people to get into the church itself. The Brazilian Jesuit style, a form of baroque, flowered in the late 17th and early 18th Centuries, when hundreds of beautiful churches, both modest and magnificent, were built. They appeared in Belém, Recife, Olinda, Bahia, Rio and, slightly later, in a last wave of baroque, in Minas Gerais. There are 13 in Ouro Prêto alone, and the many churches in the other half-deserted gold towns of Minas attest to the onetime wealth and the devoutness of the mining people.

As in Portugal, the *azulejos*—blue and white tiles—played a great part in the decoration of churches, and sometimes also in the decoration of the houses of the rich. In the towns whole house fronts were covered with these tiles, not just in blue and white but also in browns, yellows, pinks and other colors. The use of tiles for the façades of buildings has been revived in contemporary Brazilian architecture, and although the tiles are not always used very tastefully, they are an excellent finishing material in a tropical climate.

UNLIKE the overstated baroque churches seen all over Spanish America, the Brazilian churches are fundamentally simple and solid, even severe, and merely overlaid with decoration. The ornamentation grows richer through the 18th Century, with more twisted volutes, more delicate bell towers and more fanciful windows.

Much of the art and architecture of the 17th and 18th Centuries is almost as anonymous as was that of the Middle Ages in Europe, but two master sculptors and architects, both mulattoes, are known by name. Master Valentim da Fonseca e Silva studied in Europe and after his return was employed by the viceroy. He helped lay out the old Passeio Público, a waterside promenade in Rio. Most of his work has been dispersed and the park is sadly diminished, but a pair of marvelous bronze alligators still there are by "Mestre Valentim." The other sculptor, known as Aleijadinho (Little Cripple), was Antônio Francisco Lisbôa, the son of a Portuguese carpenter and a Negro slave. It is believed that Aleijadinho was a leper: he lost the use of his hands, but continued to work with tools strapped to his wrists. At the same time that the *Inconfidentes*, the idealistic revolutionaries of Minas Gerais, were dreaming of independence and producing their imitative Arcadian poetry, Aleijadinho was producing his greater and more original art. So many works—church designs, wood carvings, stone carvings—are attributed to Aleijadinho that one becomes skeptical. Nevertheless, his distinctive style can be traced all through his native region of Minas.

ALEIJADINHO'S favorite material was the gray-green soapstone of Minas, soft to cut but turning somewhat harder with exposure. It is still much used for pots and pans, and the Mineiros say that nothing is as good as a soapstone pot for cooking the daily rice. Aleijadinho's most famous works are the statues of 12 prophets that stand on the double staircase in front of the church of Bom Jesus de Matosinhos in Congonhas do Campo. Crude, but powerful and dramatic, they gesticulate against the white church with its bright blue doors and against the sweep of bare, ore-filled hills.

Throughout the 19th Century a number of fine buildings were built in Brazil, frequently adaptations of the French neoclassic style. Many of them still exist. Toward the end of the century, building deteriorated into the eclectic and fussy, tasteless imitations of architecture from all over the world.

Brazil's appreciation of its architectural heritage came late. Many early buildings were lost, beginning with the Jesuit missions abandoned after the slave-raiding expeditions of the 17th and 18th Centuries. Later, churches were sometimes deliberately torn down for their materials or to make way for street widening. The 1930s, when the modern architectural revolution began, was a period of drastic demolition, but it saw the establishment of the *Serviço do Patrimônio Histórico e Artístico Nacional*, or SPHAN, which was organized to save as many of the historical buildings of Brazil as possible. The service has since then been directed by one man, Rodrigo Mello Franco de Andrade, whose modesty, scholarship and absolute devotion to an almost hopeless task have been courageous and admirable. There is very little money available for such projects, and the average Brazilian, like his counterpart elsewhere, is indifferent to, ignorant or resentful of any interference with property. It is only natural for the inhabitants of a remote village to prefer a new gasoline station to an 18th Century fountain.

While Brazil has had fine buildings since its earliest days, it produced very little distinctive painting until the 20th Century. Some of the church-ceiling work that has survived is of fairly high quality, but it is really of interest only to the specialist. Recife, when it was held by the Dutch in the 17th Century, had its Frans Post, who did fresh and still familiar-looking landscapes while in Brazil, then spent long years in Europe painting imitations of them. With the French Mission in 1816 came illustrators of genre scenes—showing everyday life—the most notable being Jean-Baptiste Debret and Nicolas Antoine Taunay. They and others have given us volumes of fascinating, detailed studies of slaves, costumes, street scenes and buildings of the 19th Century. But most 19th Century easel painting is a dreary waste of realistic-romantic *bandeirantes*, slave girls and court functions, and landscapes that look more like France or England than Brazil. It was only with the appearance of painters such as Cândido Portinari, Lasar Segall and Emiliano di Cavalcanti in the 20th Century that Brazilian painting took on much life of its own.

PORTINARI'S early pictures are a remarkable reflection of southern Brazil's coffee country. There are the blood-red hills, the dark green coffee trees, the Negro women carrying water-filled oil cans on their heads, the children playing *futebol*. He has also done murals for public buildings in the U.S.

In Brazilian painting at present the abstract movement is triumphant, along with a minor school of it called neoconcretism. Among the best abstractionists are Aloisio Magalhães and Iberê Camargo. The Japanese-Brazilians, notably Manabu Mabe, have also made contributions to the abstract movement, but more in the Oriental calligraphic style. The best work at the moment seems to be in black and white. There are at least a dozen good engravers, woodcutters and lithographers like Fayga Ostrower, Roberto De Lamonica, Edith Behring, Anna Letycia Quadros and Maria Bonomi.

The biggest stimulus to art in recent years has been the São Paulo *Bienal*, a massive exhibition staged every other year since 1951 and modeled on the similar exhibits in Venice. Although one may have doubts about the desirability of bringing together more than 4,000 works of art at one time the show, sponsored and promoted by the São Paulo industrialist Francisco ("Cicillo") Matarazzo, has undoubtedly greatly encouraged Brazilian painting with its many prizes and its opportunities for those who have to stay at home to see at first hand, for the first time, what is being done in the rest of the world. There is a real painting boom in Brazil at present. Prices are soaring, and new galleries seem to be opening up every few weeks in all the larger cities.

SOPHISTICATED music, too, was slow to develop in Brazil, and the body of work is comparatively small. There are Indian, African and Portuguese influences at work in it, both directly and indirectly through the amazing variety of the folk music. The Jesuits had their sacred music from which many folk forms were derived, and the arrival of the Portuguese House of Braganza in 1808 proved a strong stimulus to Brazilian music. The Regent, Dom João, was charmed by the sacred compositions of the Brazilian mulatto Father José Maurício Nunes Garcia, and his own court composers enriched the musical life of the capital. Quite recently a large collection of late baroque music was discovered in Minas, and this is being transcribed and recorded. Undoubtedly much more material remains to be discovered. If and when it does come to light it should help to fill some of the long silences in Brazilian musical history.

The one major name in 19th Century Brazilian music was Carlos Gomez. Befriended all his life by Dom Pedro II, who sent him to Italy to complete his musical education, Gomez had a natural talent that is now thought to have been diluted by his overreceptiveness to Italianate influences. His most famous—though not his best—opera is *Il Guarany,* which was based on the highly romantic novel by José de Alencar about a noble Guarani Indian. It had a spectacular debut in Milan in 1870, and Gomez has the distinction of being the first New World musician to have been accepted by Europe as a "full-fledged" composer. The foyer of the great semiabandoned Manaus Opera House is decorated with a mural of a scene from *Il Guarany,* and "bife-stek Carlos Gomez" still figures on the menus of Manaus restaurants.

BLOCK PRINT by Maria Bonomi entitled "Restrained Joy" typifies the fine black-and-white work in Brazil.

The most renowned Brazilian contemporary composer is Heitor Villa-Lobos, who died in 1959. His style is rhythmic and melodic, and in his numerous operas, symphonies, concertos and other works he makes full use of the richness of Portuguese, African, Indian, folk and popular musical traditions. His contrapuntal *Bachianas Brasileiras* and his folk-influenced *Chôros* are often performed outside Brazil. Villa-Lobos also put together a manual for use in the public schools. Entitled *Guia Prático,* it uses folk songs and singing games as examples and is considered a model textbook. Other important contemporary Brazilian composers are Camargo Guarnieri and Francisco Mignone.

The poet is a special figure in Brazil, not at all like the figure who goes by the same name in the United States. There has long been a tradition in Latin countries, both European and American, of poets serving as vice consuls, consuls or ambassadors. In Brazil the word "poet" is actually a term of endearment. A man will fondly address a friend who may be an engineer or a politician as "my poet." Perhaps the custom is a relic of the days when all educated men wrote poetry; certainly the writing of poetry is commoner among Brazilians than among North Americans.

But in spite of this fondness for the *idea* of the poet as a man of special charm and privilege, writers in Brazil, unless they are employed in some government department, have professionally an even harder time of it than they would in the United States. Writing is very poorly paid and there are few fellowships and prizes. There is a mere handful of academic jobs, compared to the thousands that provide a regular income for both poets and prose writers in the United States. The writer in Brazil has to be a doctor, lawyer, engineer or journalist. There are few good magazines and reviews. Every newspaper has its weekly or daily literary page, and it is there that one has to search for the new poem, the original story or the well-written article, half lost among the essays on political and economic theory, theology and endless discussions of the French poets Charles Baudelaire or Paul Valéry, the philosopher Saint Thomas Aquinas, the essayist G. K. Chesterton or the stories of William Faulkner.

Language is, of course, a barrier between Brazilian writers and the international audience they deserve. More translations can remedy this situation for prose, but poetry is fairly impervious to successful translation, and it is a pity that most of the world remains totally ignorant of such fine contemporary poets as Manuel Bandiera (the father-figure of 20th Century Brazilian poetry), Carlos Drummond de Andrade, Cecília Meireles, Jorge de Lima, Vinícius de Morais (who wrote the play on which the successful movie *Black Orpheus* was based) and João Cabral de Mello Neto, who is probably the best of the present generation. He has written poems of great feeling about the *flagelados*, or beaten ones, as the people of the drought-stricken northeast are called.

In literature, Brazil is rediscovering some of its earlier writers. Brazilian writers can be divided roughly into those who looked to Europe, tradition and "correctness," and those who were drawn to the wilderness, the Indian and the regional. Sometimes, as in the literature of the United States, the two strains are oddly woven together.

THE poets of the *Inconfidência Mineira* sang of such un-Brazilian creatures as cupids and swans. Yet here are a few lines from the best of them, Tomás Antônio Gonzaga, which are as evocative of rural Brazil today as when they were written almost 200 years ago:

You shall not see the skillful Negro
Separate the heavy emery from the coarse sand,
And the nuggets of gold already shining,
In the bottom of the "bateia."
You shall not see the virgin forest destroyed,
Nor the burning of the still green underbrush
To fertilize the ground with ashes,
Nor the seeds being sown in the furrows.
You shall not see them rolling the black packets
Of dry leaves of fragrant tobacco,
Nor pressing out the sweet juice of the cane
Between the cog-wheels. . . .

This is a rare moment of early realism and accuracy. A *bateia* is the wooden bowl in which gold is panned. It is still used, as is the destructive slash-and-burn system of farming. Tobacco is still sold in long black coils in Brazilian markets, and sugar-cane juice, which tastes rather like a watery, grassy molasses, is still a popular drink.

Two of the outstanding characteristics of the Brazilian romantic poets of the 19th Century are their eternal *saudades* (melancholy yearnings) and their anti-slavery sentiments. Antônio Gonçalves Dias, one of the greatest of the romantics, is responsible for the "Exile's Song," written while he was a student in Portugal: "My country has palm trees/Where the *sabiá* sings/The birds don't warble here/The way they do there." Casimiro de Abreu echoes him: "If I must die in the flower of my youth/My God, let it not be now!/I want to hear the *sabiá* sing/In the evening, in the orange tree!"

The *sabiá*, a rather fat thrush, is to Brazilian poetry what the nightingale is to English verse. Carlos Gomez uses its song in the interlude of his opera *The Slave*, and 19th Century Brazilian literature is full of *sabiás*.

Brazil's most famous abolitionist poet was Antônio de Castro Alves. Lines from his long dramatic poem entitled "The Slave Ship" retain their significance and dignity to this day: "Exists a people whose banner serves / To hide such infamy and cowardice! . . . / My God, My God, what a flag is this?"

DESPITE the eminence of poets and poetry, the two greatest personalities in Brazilian literature are prose writers. Works of both are fortunately available in English. The earlier of them, Joaquim Maria Machado de Assis, is perhaps the greatest writer the South American continent has produced; some critics think he is one of the greatest of both Americas, ranking him with North America's Henry James. Born in 1839 on one of the *morros*, the hills surrounding Rio de Janeiro, the child of a poor Negro house-painter and a Portuguese woman, Machado de Assis worked as a typographer and journalist, married a middle-class Portuguese woman and over the years published book after book of poems, stories and novels. He grew famous and was highly respected and in 1897 founded the Brazilian Academy of Letters, remaining its president until his death 11 years later.

Machado de Assis is a deeply pessimistic, skeptical, reserved writer; there is little of the Latin rhetoric and nothing of its romanticism in his style. Among his best works are *Memórias póstumas de Braz Cubas* (published in English under the title of *Epitaph of a Small Winner*), *Dom Casmurro, Quincas Borba* and some of the short stories. Although the period he describes is always the latter part of the Empire and the setting is the city of Rio de Janeiro, Machado de Assis's world is universal and his characters are real people.

THE other great writer, Euclides da Cunha, was the author of one of the world's strangest books, *Os Sertões*, which was published in English as *Rebellion in the Backlands*. Da Cunha was an engineer turned war correspondent; his book is an account of military expeditions made by Brazilian troops from 1896 to 1897 in an attempt to destroy a religious fanatic, Antônio Maciel, known as *Conselheiro,* or "Counselor," who had fortified himself and all of his followers in the little settlement of Canudos, far in the interior of the state of Bahia. The *Conselheiro* and his men managed to hold out there for almost three years against repeated attacks from the government forces. The book consists partly of chronicles of futile military maneuvers, partly of dry reports of suffering and atrocities, and partly of a long geographical rhapsody. Anyone who wants to get the feel of Brazilian life and landscape at their grandiose and desperate best and worst should read *Rebellion in the Backlands*. It is reminiscent of an old Brazilian cathedral —solidly, almost crudely planned, but covered over-all with a profusion of rich ornamentation and extraneous life, to the point of being emotionally disturbing, or even repellent.

About 30 years after the publication of *Os Sertões* a new literary movement that also had its source in the hard-bitten lands of the northeast began in Brazil. Inspired by the general social awakening of the period, the "regional" novel —or novel of the proletariat—deals with the lives of the poor people, sugar-cane workers, cacao raisers, cowboys, the Negroes, as well as small-town bureaucrats and decayed landowners. The four most talented writers of this movement are Graciliano Ramos, José Lins do Rêgo, Jorge Amado and Rachel de Queiroz (see Chapter 8).

Brazil's modern movement in both art and literature owes a huge debt to Mário de Andrade, a poet who became one of the greatest forces in the country's artistic renaissance. He was interested in music, folk art, poetry and prose, and almost everything in the country's contemporary artistic life continues to benefit from his influence.

Brazil's veneration for the arts is due not only to the European tradition but also to the fact that upper-class Brazil is one big family. In spite of examples of the democracy of the arts—Aleijadinho, Machado de Assis, Mário de Andrade, all mulattoes; and Portinari, the child of poor Italian immigrants—many of the writers and artists do come from the educated and interrelated upper class. In various degrees they are all cousins, and a mutual admiration society is likely to result. It is easy to establish a reputation at an early age. But minor literary quarrels can turn into family quarrels; first names are used, even in serious articles, and everything is taken personally.

ALTHOUGH Brazilian writers and artists are spared the abrupt and cruel fluctuations of reputation that artists experience elsewhere, they probably suffer from lack of competition and serious criticism even more than from the relatively limited audience for Portuguese literature or from the deadening effects of facile journalism. A favorite way for Brazilian writers to have their pictures taken is pleasantly supine, in a fringed hammock. Too many genuine Brazilian talents seem to take to their beds too early—or to their hammocks.

On a balcony in Rio, the late composer Heitor Villa-Lobos experiments with the sounds of a crude native percussion instrument.

A Culture Stirred by New Confidence

The arts of Brazil have only recently struck root in the native soil. For four centuries the nation's artists depended largely on Europe for their standards, their fashions and even their subjects. Only in the past 50 years has their work become truly Brazilian in spirit. The distinctive traits of the nation—its racial mixtures, its restless movement and its warm tropical colors—are infusing new life into artistic endeavors that grow bolder and more self-sufficient each year.

PAINTERS have begun to win critical acclaim outside Brazil for a growing body of original works

STARK ABSTRACTIONS are painted by prize-winning Manabu Mabe (*left*), a self-taught immigrant from Japan.

BRIGHT PANELS of glass in a São Paulo art museum (*opposite*) were each done by a well-known Brazilian artist.

BITTER ALLEGORY on war by Cândido Portinari (*below*) is now a mural in UN headquarters in New York.

DESIGNERS of
daring buildings and
lush landscapes have made
the country a showplace
for spectacular architecture

MASTER GARDENER, Roberto Burle Marx (*above*) uses the rich raw materials provided by the tropics to turn the landscaping of buildings and parks into a high art.

MASTER ARCHITECT, Oscar Niemeyer (*opposite*), who is world-renowned for his lucid designs, sits on a rocky ledge inside the house he built for his family in Rio.

PACE SETTER, Lucio Costa (*right*) is the man mainly responsible for introducing architectural modernism to Brazil. He drew up the over-all city plan for Brasília.

FULL-SCALE EXHIBIT of Brazilian painting fills a wing of the exhibition hall during the 1961 *Bienal*. The art show, begun in 1951, is among the world's largest.

FIRST-NIGHT CROWDS line the balconies of the hall for the formal opening of the show (*opposite*), which offered works by 1,049 artists representing 51 nations.

Strolling to church on Sunday, a civil servant in old Rio is shown in this 19th Century print marching proudly at the head of his

household, which includes slaves dressed as finely as the family.

A Changing Social Scene

THERE is one anecdote Brazilians never tire of telling to illustrate their attitude toward race relations. When some of the ladies at Pedro II's court in the 19th Century refused to dance with a famous mulatto engineer, André Rebouças, Princess Isabel—the heiress apparent—crossed the room and asked him to dance with her. It is a nice story, and true; and it is also true that Pedro II employed several Negroes and mulattoes in high positions and that the devoted Rebouças followed him into exile and eventually died in poverty. Unfortunately this story does not necessarily prove racial tolerance, for Princess Isabel was a true princess and had been well brought up—*bem educada*, as they say.

There is a better story. In 1950, the noted dancer Katherine Dunham was turned away from one of the big hotels in São Paulo, the management remarking that it was against the hotel's policy to admit Negroes. The hotel was generally presumed to have acted as it did out of deference to the prejudices of its North American clientele. But overnight the incident became a national scandal, and although Brazil's constitution already had a clause making such discrimination a civil offense, a law was proposed (and later passed) that it would henceforth be a criminal offense. The fact that the government reacted so quickly tells much about Brazil's attitude toward the Negro.

Brazilians have great pride in their fine record in race relations. Their attitude can best be described by saying that the upper-class Brazilian is usually proud of his racial tolerance, while the lower-class Brazilian is not aware of his—he just practices it. The occasional anti-Negro or *racista* usually proves to be one of two types: the unthinking person who has come into contact with anti-Negro groups in his travels and has lost his native Brazilian tolerance; or, sadder still, the European emigrant who has come to Brazil, having suffered in his own country because of his race or poverty, and, unaccustomed to Negroes, looks down on them and is rude to them.

THE old upper class—the landed gentry, the intelligentsia, the diplomatic set and a few other groups—resents the small, pushing new upper class—mainly first and second generation immigrants who have made their fortunes in business and industry. Nostalgic for the old days when the class system was more rigid, they look down on what they consider the lack of education and social graces of the new rich; yet the two groups are gradually merging and forming a new segment of society. Their ranks are being joined continually by members of the professional and white-collar middle class, who in turn are subjected to the same resentments as they attempt to move up. At the bottom of the scale the "poor" whites, Negroes and mulattoes are treated with a combination of warmth and intimacy on the one hand, and an autocratic manner on the other.

Such discrimination as does exist is based on economic, social or educational grounds rather than on racial ones. The country has no anti-Semitism. A young Jewish business man of Brazil, intelligent but not well-read or well-traveled, was astounded, when planning his first trip to the United States, to be warned about "restricted" hotels. The idea of being discriminated against because he had a Jewish name had never occurred to him.

It is true that the Negro or mulatto in Brazil is usually a second-class citizen, rarely found in important positions or even good jobs and almost always poor. But since most of the population is in exactly the same situation and suffers the same deprivations, the Negro's sufferings do not mark him out as being very different from anyone else. Negroes have equal opportunity and education, even if that does not mean much yet; and in the arts there is no discrimination whatsoever. Three of the greatest and most admired figures in the arts have been mulattoes: the sculptor "Aleijadinho," the writer Machado de Assis and the poet Mario de Andrade.

The widespread poverty, backwardness, ignorance and suffering in Brazil is tragic; for millions, life is hungry and dirty, short and cruel. And yet to any liberal-minded South African or North American, for example, it comes as a revelation to hear, as one can in Brazil, a black cook calling her elderly, white mistress *minha negrinha*, "my little nigger," as a term of affection.

Such an attitude was not planned; it just happened. But Brazil is now realizing that its history of racial assimilation is one of the country's greatest assets. Racial mixtures can be seen all over the country. With each new census, an increasing proportion of the total population is classified as white.

THE Portuguese have naturally constituted the largest group of immigrants to Brazil, and they still come in at the rate of 17,000 a year. The recent arrivals generally become laborers, farmers, servants or gardeners. Also, certain ancient city trades are theirs: they are knife grinders, or dealers in old newspapers and bottles. In the cities a great deal of freight is pushed about on handcarts and this too is the prerogative of the Portuguese. The actual official name for these handcart men is *burros sem rabos*, or "donkeys without tails." Their usual costume is wooden clogs, wide trousers, undershirts and large floppy berets, and their faces are handsome and stolid compared to the often ugly but more subtle and mobile faces of Brazilians of several generations' standing.

In endless jokes the Portuguese peasant is always shown as absurdly literal-minded and naive. In the 19th and early 20th Century Brazilian theater, the middle-class Portuguese was represented as a loudly dressed bumpkin, given to big gold watches and heavy watch-chains. In Portugal at the same period, on the other hand, the "colonial" who had lived in Brazil and had returned was being represented on the stage the same way.

AFTER the abolition of slavery other European immigrants besides the Portuguese started to arrive in large numbers. They went mostly to the states of São Paulo, Santa Catarina, Rio Grande do Sul and Paraná. Germans, Italians and, after 1908, Japanese all poured in. There are whole towns and villages in the south that are dominated by Germans. The Japanese originally came in following an agreement between the São Paulo state government and a colonizing company in Japan to help develop the São Paulo interior; at present there are about half a million of them in Brazil, and they contribute enormously to the improvement of agriculture, particularly in the vegetable and fruit-growing areas of the southern states. São Paulo has Japanese grocery stores, bookshops and even geisha girls. The five million people of Italian descent have adapted themselves best of all, probably because the climate and working conditions in Brazil are not unlike those in Italy, and Portuguese is an easy language for them to learn. But new groups continue to arrive in Brazil, most notably the Levantines, who now number more than 400,000.

Brazil's most fascinating minority group, however, is made up by the half a million or so Indians, whose protection and well-being the Brazilian government has for many years tried to ensure. The founder and hero of the Indian Protection Service was Marshal Cândido Mariano da Silva Rondon, who came from Cuiabá, capital of the state of Mato Grosso, and was himself part Indian. As a major in the Brazilian army in 1907, Rondon was given the task of building a telegraph line to link Mato Grosso with Pôrto Velho on the Madeira River and with the outside world. This meant exploring thousands of square miles of wilderness for the first time. Rondon's story is one of heroism and self-sacrifice. He believed that the Indians should and could be "pacified," even though many Brazilians were for exterminating them. The motto he gave to the service was, "Die if necessary, but never kill"—and many of Rondon's men did just that. He tried never to interfere with the Indians' way of life.

Just before World War I, Theodore Roosevelt went on an exploring expedition with Rondon. He paid high tribute to Rondon in his book *Through the Brazilian Wilderness*, which probably brought Brazil to the attention of more Americans than anything since Dom Pedro II's visit in 1876. Before Rondon died in 1958, he had discovered 15 major rivers (naming one for Roosevelt), built more than 15,000 miles of telegraph lines and found many previously unknown tribes of Indians.

Today there are occasional news stories of land-greedy men who cheat or murder the Indians and of sad publicity stunts involving them, but Rondon set a high standard of behavior toward primitive man. The territory of Rondônia (larger than the whole of Great Britain) is named for him.

RONDON'S heir as the principal benefactor of the Indians is Orlando Villas Boas, who has dedicated his life to the jungle people. He has spent years at remote posts, out of touch with civilization, and much prefers living with the Indians to being an administrator. But the Indians continue to be a problem, almost a hopeless one. Tribes that have never seen the white man's civilization are still being discovered, while those that have come in contact with it are dying off in disease and degradation. Sometimes the problem is a dangerous one. Recently the body of a young English explorer was found, pierced by seven arrows identified as having come from the Cayapó Indians. Nor are explorers the only ones threatened. The isolated rubber grower or cattle raiser of Mato Grosso or Pará, even though he lives in the nuclear age, still has more to fear from arrows or blowpipes than from bombs.

ONE night on board a ship going down the muddy Amazon a young woman doctor was telling stories. She had been 15 years with the *Serviço Especial de Saúde Pública*, the Special Public Health Service which was founded jointly by the United States and Brazil in 1942 and taken over completely by Brazil in 1960. She was 23 when she entered the S.E.S.P.; she had gone up to Santarém, then another hundred miles or so by launch, and landed with her instruments and a few books to start her career at a small village on the Rio Tapajós. The first night a group of wild, ragged men asked her to make out the death certificate of a fellow villager whose body had just been found in the river. The villagers said the man had been drowned. The doctor asked to be left alone with the body and found that, although it had been in the water for some time, the man had died of a stab in the back. Quite alone, at night and with the knowledge that the murderer (or murderers) must be in the group of threatening men, she refused to sign the death warrant and ordered someone to go for the nearest police representative, half a day's trip by motor boat. And she got it done.

Small, animated and dark, probably with Indian blood, this doctor was a "modern" Brazilian woman. There are not many like her, but there are a few and the numbers are increasing.

Brazil is a man's country. The double standard could scarcely be more taken for granted. Little boys are spoiled (or so an Anglo-Saxon would say), and everything within the home revolves around the head of the house or the son of the family, often referred to simply as "the man." In this man's world, women are classified as "the mother of my children" or "the bearer of my name."

But nothing is that simple. Even if poor women trail behind the men, carrying the baby in their arms and the water jug on their heads, things have changed a great deal since the first Portuguese carried off the Indian girls. In the old days women were scarce and were kept in harem-like seclusion, peering out at the world through *muxarabiês* or lattice windows, or from the *alcovas* or inner rooms of the old farmhouses. For 300 years they were rarely taught to read or write, and as young as 12 years old they were married off to neighbors, cousins and even uncles. There are true stories of little girls being given dolls as bribes for marrying much older men. All the early travelers speak of the timidity of Brazilian women and the rarity with which they were seen by male guests. They grew white and fat in the darkened rooms, rarely walking, swaying in hammocks or sitting cross-legged on pillows and attending to household affairs, while their husbands, according to most accounts, made merry in the slave quarters. What seemed like an indolent life was in reality a responsible one, and the wife would be managing the vast household, sitting on her cushions, sewing, issuing a stream of orders all day long.

IT is only in the last hundred years that women in Brazil have received anything approaching a formal education, and even today lower-class girls, who are less well off in this respect than boys, are lucky if they get as much as a year or two of school. Upper-class girls go to convent schools, some good, some bad. In spite of the general Brazilian kindliness, too many upper-class women still treat their servants or social inferiors in the old 18th Century manner and let their children grow up doing the same thing.

Since women have been for the most part illiterate for so many generations, naturally there have been almost no women writers. We can learn the women's side of 19th Century life from visitors like the Englishwoman Maria Graham, or from the letters of the many foreign governesses employed by well-to-do Brazilians. Some of the talent that was wasted can be imagined by reading such a book as the *Diary of Helena Morley*, an authentic journal kept in Diamantina in the 1890s by a teenage girl who certainly had enough talent to become a first-rate novelist.

But women are now prominent in Brazilian letters. Cecília Meireles is one of Brazil's best poets, and Clarice Lispector is a short-story writer and novelist of considerable originality. There are many others. The best known of all is Rachel de Queiroz, who at the age of 19 wrote a short, brilliant novel about the state of Ceará called *The '15*, describing the year of a particularly dreadful drought. She came to Rio and wrote novels, and for many years she has had a page in *O Cruzeiro*, Brazil's biggest weekly picture magazine, in which she has consistently and courageously fought for political and social causes. In 1961, President Quadros invited her to be Minister of Education. She declined, but it was the first time in Brazil a woman had been so honored. There are now women in the government and in Congress, and there are women lawyers, doctors, psychoanalysts and engineers. Odete de Carvalho has been ambassadress to Israel and Costa Rica.

DESPITE the advances that have been made, women in Brazil have not yet achieved the status they have in other countries. Marriage is still customary at 17 or 18, and even the rich and educated often can look forward only to a life of child-rearing. Women themselves are often opposed to introducing divorce, since security for themselves and for their children is the most important thing of all to them.

Although women got the vote in Brazil in 1932, they still do not have full legal rights. They usually think as their husbands do. They accept their husbands' infidelities as a matter of course. Some of them will insist that they are happier than North American women—but that is usually after they have visited the United States and seen how American women do so much of their own work without servants, take care of their own children, support themselves, or are otherwise rushed and harassed.

IN this country where so much is changing, another new development is mass spectator sports. Of these, by far the most popular is *futebol* (soccer). Only 30 years ago, *futebol* was a strictly amateur affair, played by members of the upper classes. Now, like baseball in the United States, it is a big business, with high salaries, the buying and selling of players and national heroes. Every newspaper devotes at least a page to it every day, and important matches generate an excitement that borders on the hysterical. The players are all shades from white to jet black, graceful, nervous and incredibly quick, and they rank among the best in the world. For years, however, international glory eluded them; each time a crucial match came up, the players seemed to lose all sense of team play. Finally in 1958 the Brazilian team, accompanied by a dentist and a psychologist among other specialists, journeyed to Sweden and won the world title. Their welcome back to Rio was tumultuous.

In the country on Sundays, the population of every small village will be out watching the local *futebol* teams. The big pale-green fields are edged with people in their Sunday best, holding their babies and carrying umbrellas against the sun. There is the *kibon* or ice cream man with his yellow wagon, and the spun-sugar man with his homemade wagon mounted on a tricycle. Buzzards and delicate tissue-paper kites poise high overhead and the players in their brilliantly striped jerseys and brief shorts are running, running.

It is also a common sight to see the local washerwoman's line hung with the jerseys of one team, sweaters striped like wasps—a cheerful display—sometimes against the background of a city dump, with more buzzards and more paper kites hovering above it.

Talents to Match a New Complexity

A country becoming steadily more urban and more industrialized, Brazil has outgrown the talents of its old ruling class. The country's free politics demands an informed electorate and its factories require trained technicians.

Such needs are being met slowly. The rural population remains dangerously illiterate. But in the cities a growing number of fine secondary schools are training the new middle class for the critical role it will play in the new Brazil.

EXPECTANT NEWSBOY hawks his papers in a market in Bahia (*opposite*). Brazil has numerous daily newspapers, but less than half of the population is literate.

CONVENIENT NEWSSTAND in São Paulo strings up its newspapers for browsers. Avidly read, Brazil's better papers feature highly influential discussions of politics.

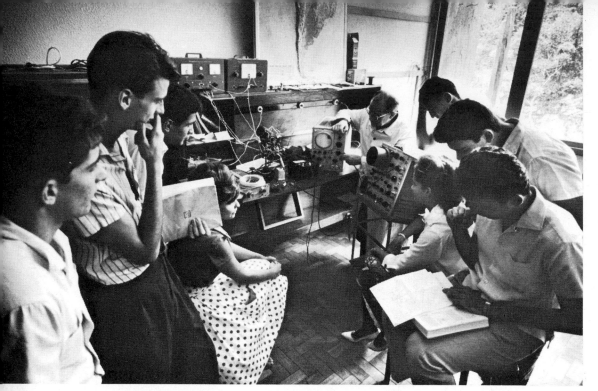

STUDYING INTENTLY, college-level students at a physics institute (*above*) learn to use an oscillograph. Scientific training is now a key part of higher education.

PLAYING INFORMALLY in the well-equipped yard of a Catholic school in Rio (*right*), young boys take time out from course work that includes four years of languages.

DRAWING VIGOROUSLY, children at a government-run art school (*below*) are encouraged to express themselves in classes that supplement their regular course of study.

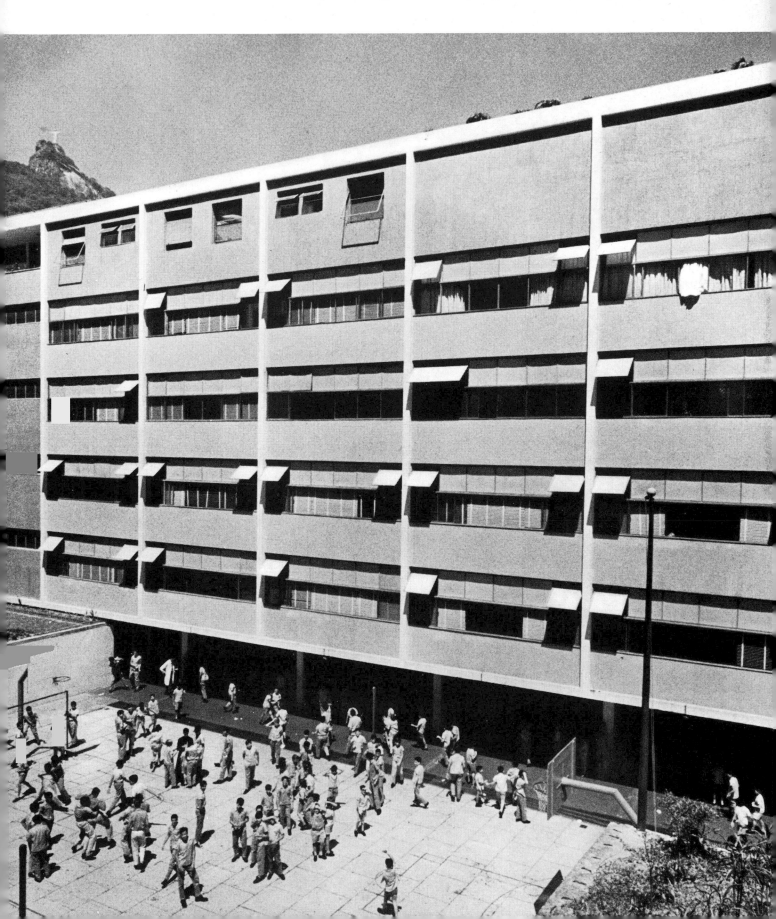

CATHOLICISM is the prevailing faith, though the Church is not a powerful establishment

HUMBLE OFFERINGS of candles are made on All Souls' Day at a church grotto in Rio. Despite its 65.5 million adherents, the Catholic Church perennially lacks priests.

GOLDEN EBULLIENCE of the 250-year-old Church of São Francisco de Assis in Bahia testifies to the largess of the sugar barons, on whom the local clergy depended.

SOCCER has become a wildly popular professional sport whose stars are national heroes

IMPORTANT MATCH between Hungarians and Brazilians (*above*) draws 130,000 fans to the stadium in Rio.

TOP PLAYER, Edson ("Pelé") Arantes do Nascimento (*opposite*) stars for Santos and takes in $47,000 a year.

WORLD CHAMPIONS in 1958, Brazil's soccer team (*below*) rides triumphantly through Rio on a fire truck.

Struggle for a Stable Democracy

THE people of the United States of Brazil have long wanted a democracy. But many factors have prevented the country from achieving stable, democratic government. Democracy in the contemporary world demands, among other things, an educated and informed people. Up until now Brazil has not had one. Illiteracy, slow communications and a consequent lack of awareness among the people have made it possible for determined groups of men to control the affairs of the country without the general consent—or even the knowledge—of the Brazilian people as a whole. The military in Brazil, unlike the military in other South American countries, have never wanted permanent power. On the occasions they have seized power, they have never kept it for long. But Brazil did suffer from a dictatorship. From 1930 to 1945 and from 1951 to 1954, one man, Getúlio Vargas, ran the country as president, dictator, or both. The large group of power-craving men who were his followers and the political machinery he helped set up have done the country inestimable damage.

Not only did Brazil lose ground politically because of Vargas, but Vargas did little to increase respect for government. When he entered office, there was hope that he would broaden participation in government and make long-needed reforms. Yet today as always, the government in general is mistrusted, taxes are evaded and in political matters an atmosphere of suspicion and cynicism prevails. President Jânio Quadros, a non-Vargas man who was elected in 1960 only to turn in a sudden resignation after seven months in office, briefly gave the country new hope. That hope too failed. Brazil has since been trying desperately to find a way ahead.

IN order to understand what produced the Vargas regime and the contemporary Brazilian political atmosphere, it is necessary to examine the forces which dominated the republic in its earliest days. After the overthrow of the Empire in 1889 (see Chapter 3), the old republic started as an improvised collaboration of ill-assorted elements: the Positivist group that dreamed of establishing a political utopia; the military group led by the first president, Marshal Manuel Deodoro da Fonseca; and the great landowners, many of whom had been ruined by the abolition of slavery. It was a chance collaboration, bound to break up; and it did almost immediately.

The Positivists were the first to disassociate themselves from the new government. The world of practical politics was very different from what they had imagined. "This is not the republic of our dreams!" they complained, and departed, leaving only their slogan *Order and Progress* on the Brazilian flag. Marshal Deodoro went next. In spite of having proclaimed the new republic, he was reluctant to give up his power as an old imperial marshal. He disagreed with many of his former associates and, facing both armed rebellion and strong opposition in Congress, he attempted a military coup (or *golpe*, as Brazilians call it), dissolved Congress and ended by renouncing his office —an example of the Brazilian habit of simply walking out of office without much warning when hampered by strong opposition.

The terms of his immediate successors were scarcely quieter. The presidency of the "Iron Marshal," Floriano Peixoto, who succeeded Deodoro in 1891, was disturbed by a rebellion of naval officers and by civil war in the south. The next president was a civilian from São Paulo, Prudente José de Moraes Barros. During his term the one "religious war" in Brazilian history took place, the small but macabre and bloody war of Canudos. A mad mystic named Antônio Maciel, called *Conselheiro* or "Counselor," appeared in the backlands of Bahia and attracted a large following of religious fanatics. At first the *Conselheiro's* movement was purely religious: prayers, penances and pilgrimages of the ever-growing band through the arid wastes of the *caatinga*, or scrub-forest land. Then the *Conselheiro* announced a new dogma: the rule of the republic was the rule of the Antichrist, and his followers should fight for the return of the monarchy.

A long struggle began. At first the government thought that a small-scale police operation could stop the *Conselheiro's* movement. But his followers put up such fanatic resistance in their stronghold at Canudos that the operation assumed almost the proportions of civil war. After severe losses, the government organized a full-scale expedition, and in 1897 Canudos and its defenders were destroyed.

ALTHOUGH the young republic had yet to produce a body of statesmen, matters gradually improved. Inevitably the men of the Empire—generally referred to as "Counselors," because many of them had held that title under the Empire—came back to power. It was not surprising. They were more gifted and better prepared for the task.

While the economy remained primarily agricultural, the cities began to expand. With the slogan of "Civilize Rio," the old capital of Dom João VI began to open up avenues and install port facilities and to lose its provincial atmosphere. Sanitary measures virtually wiped out yellow fever, long the scourge of the city. The citizens had called the disease "the patriot" because it seemed to show a preference for foreigners resident in the city. An inoculation campaign destroyed the horror of smallpox.

Under the Counselors, the country was briefly stabilized. Money was sound and coffee held sway. But there was little basic change in the nature of the governmental system. Following imperial tradition, the presidents kept the Congress a subsidiary of the executive power. As always, the big states dominated the smaller, and two of them—São Paulo and Minas Gerais—dominated all the rest. The presidency was alternated between men from one or the other state. Since São Paulo was famous for its coffee and Minas Gerais was renowned for its vast cattle ranches and dairy products, this political arrangement was popularly called "coffee and milk," after *cafe com leite,* the usual Brazilian breakfast drink.

DURING and after World War I, educated Brazilians, influenced by the wave of social agitation the war produced, began to feel an urgent necessity for social and political reforms, particularly election reforms, since without universal suffrage democracy was in reality just a phrase. Such feelings were shared by many army officers, who traditionally regarded themselves as the guardians of public morality, and it was in the army that real trouble began.

The year 1922 was the first centenary of independence, celebrated with extensive public festivities. On the 5th of July, rebellious and idealistic young officers of Rio's Copacabana Fort dismissed their own troops and marched out alone to face the government forces. Almost all of the young officers—known as "the 18 of Copacabana"—were killed on the spot, but the march was the first serious episode of rebellion. Two years later, on the anniversary of the 5th of July march of the "18 of Copacabana," a revolution broke out in São Paulo.

The São Paulo rebels' chief complaints, like those of the rebel officers, were that the republic was too bureaucratic and that it had yet to rid itself of the conservative oligarchs of the plantations and ranches, the old families of the interior. In the cities new groups—laborers, small businessmen and professionals—were

arising, and being ignored. Out of this second "5th of July" of 1924 grew a movement of rebellion that was to help upset the old republic. The rebellious troops, driven back to Rio Grande do Sul, began one of the most dramatic movements in the history of Brazil.

ABOUT 2,000 men, soldiers and civilians, had refused to surrender to the government. They were headed by a group of officers who have since all left their marks on Brazilian history. The leader was Luiz Carlos Prestes, who later became chief of the Brazilian Communists. The Prestes column left Rio Grande do Sul and for more than two years made its way through the interior of Brazil, through lands at that time not even mapped. In general, the population received Prestes' men with sympathy. Prestes himself, dubbed "Knight of Hope," became a legendary figure. After trekking thousands of miles in the hinterlands, the column split into two parts, one finding asylum in Bolivia, the other in Argentina.

In 1930 the president was Washington Luiz Pereira de Souza, from São Paulo. But instead of keeping to the "coffee and milk" understanding and allowing himself, a "coffee" man, to be followed by "milk"—a president from Minas Gerais—he succeeded in getting another Paulista nominated as his successor. The powerful state of Minas resented this tipping of the scales in favor of the rival state and aligned itself with the ever-present rebellious military elements. As their candidate the Minas politicians nominated Getúlio Vargas, governor of Rio Grande do Sul. Promising sweeping reforms, Vargas won the support of the exiled officers and of large groups of students, workers and professionals. But when the ballots were counted, Vargas was declared the loser. Revolt began.

An army junta seized control of the capital and expelled Washington Luiz, while insurrectionary troops marched toward it from north and south. One by one, the state governors were pushed out by the rebel forces. One of Vargas' emissaries hinted to the junta in Rio that the revolutionary armies would attack the capital if power was not turned over to Vargas. The junta capitulated. Vargas marched triumphantly into the capital and was sworn in as president of a provisional government. The Vargas era had arrived. To those who had supported him, President Vargas appeared to be the man who would carry out all the long-wanted reforms.

IMMEDIATE elections were promised, but the new president kept putting them off. The state of São Paulo, although the richest in Brazil, was humiliated by the conquerors, who handed it over to the mercies of the "officers" of the revolution. In 1932, under the slogan of "Constitutionalization," the Paulistas took up arms. The rest of the country did not support them, and Vargas, in control of the army, crushed the revolt.

The pressure of the opposition, however, forced Vargas to grant permission for a Constituent Assembly. In 1934 the Assembly voted a new constitution, which incorporated many of the demands of the revolutionaries of 1922, 1924 and 1930—the secret ballot, female suffrage and the representation of all classes in government. Then the Assembly elected Vargas president of the new republic for a term of four years. For a time it appeared that the liberals and the revolutionary leaders had triumphed. But Vargas, the "strong man" of the frontier, did not care for the restrictions the new constitution placed on him, and in 1935 the opportunity he had been waiting for arrived. The Communists promoted a united front movement of leftists, under the name of Alliance of National Liberation. Led by Luiz Carlos Prestes, who had become a Communist after a period spent in Russia, they succeeded in stirring up revolution in Rio and in the northeast. Vargas decreed a "state of siege" and quickly put down the revolt.

Protected by his "state of siege" powers, he then secretly ordered his advisers to draw up a new constitution, sent advance emissaries to all the states to guarantee the support of the governors, and jailed intellectuals and politicians who carried any weight with the public. On the 10th of November 1937, in a surprise move, he surrounded the two houses of Congress with troops, closed them and put his secret constitution into effect. Vargas was now the undisguised dictator of Brazil.

The idea of dictatorship was intolerable to the majority of Brazilians. Yet the Brazilian form did not take on the worst aspects of European dictatorship. Opponents of the regime tauntingly called it "Fascism Brazilian-style," or "Fascism with sugar." Individual rights were curtailed, there were arbitrary arrests and the press was controlled. But there were no public executions, no shootings, no concentration camps. After the first few months most of the political prisoners were released; only a few leaders remained in jail. Others were allowed to go into exile. In 1938, Brazil's extreme right-wing party, the *Integralistas*, attempted an uprising. Their forces surrounded the presidential palace and attempted to assassinate Vargas. Rescued by the army, Vargas put down the revolt. The leader of the *Integralistas* was then also permitted to go into exile.

Getúlio (Brazilian political leaders are usually known by their first names) was an opportunist and a shrewd politician, and he made himself beloved by the Brazilian masses. He set up unions in the city factories and established a minimum wage and a maximum work week. His social security program was an advanced one on paper, but few benefits from it ever reached the workers.

IT was World War II which helped bring about Vargas' downfall as dictator. At the start of the war it was not apparent where his sympathies lay; he made friendly gestures to both sides. But after the sinking of Brazilian merchant ships by Nazi submarines prompted a series of campaigns in the newspapers and demonstrations in the streets, Vargas declared war against the Axis. Brazil ceded naval and air bases to the U.S. From Natal large numbers of troops and quantities of supplies were airlifted across the Atlantic to Dakar in West Africa. A Brazilian division fought with the American 5th Army in Italy.

It was scarcely possible to maintain the authoritarian "New State," as Vargas called his regime, after the enthusiasm Brazil had shown for the Allies and its own returning soldiers. The United States put discreet pressure on Vargas to permit free elections. The press began to disobey the government censorship, and Vargas was unable to reimpose it. In October 1945 the ranking military officers, realizing that the dictatorship was tottering, ordered Vargas out and exiled him to his far-off *fazenda* in Rio Grande do Sul.

IT was high time. After 15 years of Getúlio, Brazil was still in debt and industrially undeveloped. The dignity of Brazil and that of many an individual Brazilian had been affronted by his dictatorship. The record, however, was not entirely bad. By establishing steel mills at Volta Redonda with U.S. aid granted during the war, Vargas had laid the foundations of his country's future industrialization.

After Vargas' ouster, elections were held. The anti-Vargas forces nominated Air Brigadier General Eduardo Gomes, popular as the only remaining survivor of the "18 of Copacabana" of 1922. But Vargas' political machine still functioned, even without him, and the leaders of the "New State" remained in power. Their candidate, General Eurico Gaspar Dutra, Vargas' ex-Minister of War who had been called the "Constable of the New State," was elected.

Surprisingly enough, Dutra showed respect for the liberal new constitution which had been promulgated after Vargas' departure and displayed no tendency to seek personal power or permit military excesses. But the necessary electoral reforms were not made, and Vargas' political rights were not revoked. In 1950 when Dutra's term was up, Getúlio ran again for the presidency. With his old machine working smoothly and with a nationwide high-pressure campaign, the like of which had never been seen in Brazil, he won by an impressive plurality and thus became the lawfully elected president.

Times had changed, however. Dutra had governed honestly and respected the law. The group that returned to power with Vargas was eager for power, fame and money. Getúlio was surrounded by corruption so deep that when he became aware of its extent, he himself referred to it as "the sea of mud." (Vargas was believed to be honest but out of touch, isolated by his own entourage.) Outspoken critics fought bitterly against Vargas and "Getúlismo." Carlos Lacerda, publisher of the newspaper *Tribuna da Imprensa,* was his best-known opponent, exposing graft and chicanery in government circles and even among the members of Vargas' own family. Members of Vargas' bodyguard attempted to assassinate Lacerda. A young air force major, Rubens Florentino Vaz, acting as a bodyguard for Lacerda, was killed; Lacerda escaped with a bullet in the foot.

THIS political murder understandably produced a national scandal. Lacerda publicly accused the president's son of having instigated the crime. It was later proved, however, that Getúlio and his son were both ignorant of the entire affair. The air force tracked down the man responsible for the major's death—the head of the presidential bodyguard—and a group of air force officers arrested him in the presidential palace itself. High-ranking members of the armed forces then demanded the president's resignation in a dramatic scene in the early morning of August 24, 1954. Vargas, still in pajamas, apparently agreed to resign; he retired to his bedroom—and shot himself through the heart. He left behind an extraordinary letter whose authenticity is to this day disputed in Brazil. It attests to his good works on behalf of the country, and warns darkly against international forces.

Vargas' immediate successor was the vice-president, João Café Filho. After completing Vargas' term, President Café was succeeded in 1956 by Juscelino Kubitschek, ex-governor of Minas Gerais and a Vargas man. Kubitschek had won the election with the assistance of the

Vargas machine. When the victory—although legal—was questioned, a group of top military leaders briefly seized power through a *golpe preventivo* in an effort to uphold the constitution. Declaring the country in a state of siege, they guaranteed Kubitschek's inauguration and then withdrew from the scene.

In office Kubitschek showed no rancor. He was hyperactive, optimistic and ambitious, and boasted that the country would achieve "50 years in five." He undertook his great work, the building of the new capital of Brasília. Under Kubitschek industrialization began in earnest: iron ore exports were doubled and a Brazilian automobile industry was started. He began an ambitious highway program and undertook the construction of great dams in order to increase the country's supply of electrical power. But the Kubitschek government was susceptible to corruption and graft. Some Brazilians contended that the corruption even exceeded that of the Vargas days. Control of the country remained in the hands of a few powerful political and economic groups. While the south remained rich and prosperous, the northeast was still abysmally poor. Inflation, which had begun in the days of Vargas, now increased at nightmare rates—in part as a result of the rapid industrialization. It was estimated that Kubitschek spent $600 million on Brasília. In short, the chronic problems of the country remained unsolved. Yet Kubitschek's development program had set Brazil on a course from which there could be no turning, and which in time could bring a greater measure of wealth to all its citizens.

The candidate of the still-strong Vargas group in the 1960 election was General Henrique Lott, one of the generals of the *golpe preventivo* that had helped insure Kubitschek's inauguration in 1956. The other candidate was the ex-governor of the state of São Paulo, Jânio Quadros, a 43-year-old former teacher whose political career had been meteoric. As governor of São Paulo, Quadros had cleared out graft, balanced the budget, tripled the highway mileage and begun a dam-building program with a potential power output exceeding all of the Brazilian national capacity.

Quadros said that he was the "new broom" which would forever sweep away the corruption of the Vargas and Kubitschek eras; his campaign badge was a miniature broom. In the biggest election ever held in Brazil, he was elected by a tremendous plurality of 1.7 million votes. When he entered office in 1961, there was a new atmosphere in Brazil. The people wanted change, wanted morality in government and even wanted austerity. They wanted anything that would allow them escape from spiraling inflation and the long years of government corruption and waste. Brazil was hopeful at last.

And at first all went well. As he had in his home state of São Paulo, Quadros ordered investigations into graft and fired superfluous government workers. He was equally energetic in other areas. He set up a one-billion-dollar highway program and two billion dollars' worth of hydroelectric projects. He announced plans to step up education in the primary schools with the goal of increasing literacy from 48 per cent to 70 per cent in five years, and programs to double steel production and develop other industries. Other Quadros policies, however, particularly proposals for tax and land reform,

VARGAS' SUICIDE LETTER

... Once again the forces that are coordinated by the interests against the people have anew unleashed themselves over me.... They need to gag my voice and prevent my action, so that I will not continue to defend the people.... After decades of domination and exploitation by international economic-financial groups, I made myself the chief of a revolution, and I won. I initiated the work of liberation and ... a regime of social liberty.... I can give nothing further but my blood.... I choose this way to be always with you.... I gave you my life. Now I offer my death.... Serenely, I take the first step on the road to eternity and I leave life to enter history.

ran into strong resistance from his opposition congress. In addition, there was considerable public uproar when Quadros awarded the Order of the Southern Cross, Brazil's highest decoration for foreigners, to Ernesto ("Che") Guevara, the Communist-leaning economics minister of Cuba. Quadros came under increasing attacks from Carlos Lacerda, who had become the governor of the state of Guanabara, the former federal district in which the city of Rio is situated. At the same time Quadros began sounding out leaders of the Congress on the possibility of his being granted additional powers—a request to which Congress was flatly opposed. Late in August Lacerda reported in a speech carried on television and radio that he had been approached by Quadros' Minister of Justice and that Quadros was planning to take additional power. Lacerda is a controversial man, but his honesty is unquestioned. The speech created a national sensation.

On the morning of August 25, Quadros had a letter of resignation ready.

QUADROS' RESIGNATION NOTE

... I have been beaten . . . and so I leave the Government. . . . I have carried out my duty. . . . But unfortunately all my efforts were in vain to lead this nation in the direction of its true economic and political freedom. . . . I wanted Brazil for Brazilians and because I had to face and fight corruption, lies and cowardliness, whose only goals are to subject the general needs of the nation to some ambitious groups and individuals from inside and also from outside.

However, I feel crushed. Terrible forces came forward to fight me and to defame me. . . . Here I close this page of my life and of the national history. . . .

The heads of the army, navy and air force hurried to the palace and begged him not to resign. Quadros was adamant. He sent the letter to Congress and flew to Cumbica, the military airport near the city of São Paulo. His letter, like the one allegedly left by Vargas seven years earlier, hinted at threats from mysterious foreign powers and claimed devotion to the interests of Brazil and its people. He waited for five hours in the plane, evidently expecting to be recalled, but was not. Congress accepted his resignation.

Thus began the most serious crisis in recent Brazilian history. The vice-president, who according to the constitution would now become president, was João "Jango" Goulart. A Vargas protégé who still controlled the Brazilian Labor party which Vargas had founded, he was regarded as demagogic, opportunistic, leftist and a political uncertainty. At the time of Quadros' resignation, he had just left Communist China, where he had been arranging a Brazilian-Chinese trade pact. He was unacceptable to the heads of the armed forces, who announced that he would be arrested on his return to Brazil. In Rio troops were ordered into the streets. Censors took over press, radio and television. While Goulart returned to his country by cautious stages, his supporters in his home state of Rio Grande do Sul, where his brother-in-law was governor, prepared for a fight. Thirteen days of uncertainty followed. But there was strong sentiment for the preservation of the constitution.

After considerable maneuvering behind scenes, Congress passed a constitutional amendment that changed the government from a presidential system like that of the U.S. to a parliamentary system akin to that of West Germany. (It was immediately called "the bi-focal government.") A prime minister was made the new executive head of the government and the president's powers were reduced. Goulart was duly sworn in and, with the approval of Congress, chose Tancredo Neves as the new prime minister. Neves had been Minister of Justice in the Vargas cabinet.

The crisis was averted, and Brazil had again displayed its great "talent for compromise"— a phrase frequently used by Brazilians themselves even though, like the phrase "land of unfulfilled promise," it is beginning to get on their nerves.

LAST CEREMONY as president is performed by Jânio Quadros (*left*) for a soldiers' day celebration on August 25, 1961. Shortly after, he announced his resignation.

LAST MOMENTS in Brazil are spent by Quadros (*right*) on shipboard waiting to sail for England. He had hoped in vain for a last-minute plea that he come back to office.

The Pains of Political Growth

The upsurge of mass democracy is one of the chief causes of the crisis in Brazilian politics. Until Getúlio Vargas showed that a man could gain power by a bold appeal to the people, the masses were of small account in the old gentlemanly game of politics. Today the old political scene is fading, but the new democratic one is still confused. The electorate is inexperienced and demagoguery is rampant, and the political parties too often lack clear-cut programs. These are serious problems, but in the long view they represent a stage in a free people's political growth.

PEACEFUL SOLUTION to a crisis verging on

civil war was arrived at through drastic compromise

TALKING WITH FRIENDS, President Goulart smiles as the 13-day crisis ends on September 7, 1961. Overnight, Brazil had adopted a parliamentary form of government.

NEWLY ARRIVED in Brazil, the new leftist president João Goulart (*left*) enters the presidential office building. To reduce his authority Congress changed the constitution.

POLITICAL FORCES are split

into numerous parties and

factions which often group themselves

around a few strong personalities

INFLUENTIAL POPULIST, ex-President Juscelino Kubitschek (*above*) had the support of both the pro-labor and conservative branches of the old Vargas coalition.

MILITARY CONSERVATIVE, Marshal Odilio Denys signs a book (*right*) in a 1960 ceremony making him Minister of War. He led the forces opposing Goulart as president.

DYNAMIC CRUSADER, Governor Carlos Lacerda has long combatted left-wing elements and all forms of dictatorship through his daily newspaper *Tribuna da Imprensa*.

THE BLIGHT of poverty,

increasing in spite

of industrial growth,

is taxing the capabilities

of free institutions

VERTICAL SLUMS, the *favelas* of Rio are home to almost a million people, who live without running water or sewers literally a stone's throw from Rio's luxury apartment houses. Flimsy shanties built of odd scraps, they are inhabited mainly by rural people who come to Rio to find work. Although the *favelas* are no worse than many other city slums, they are more conspicuous—inescapable reminders of the rural squalor behind Brazil's industrial progress.

MESSIANIC LEADER, Francisco Julião meets with sugar-cane workers in Pernambuco. His Peasant League movement demands the breakup of the region's huge estates.

PRO-CASTRO RALLY organized in Recife by the Peasant League (*opposite*) attracts a small but militant turnout of laborers, who were harangued by anti-U.S. speakers.

VELVETY DUSK drapes Rio
and Sugar Loaf Mountain.
To the west lies the hinterland, still mysterious enough
to encourage Brazilians with
dreams of future prosperity.

10

A Nation Perplexed and Uncertain

THE strange defection of President Jânio Quadros brought another political crisis to Brazil. The new form of government, *parliamentarismo*, seemed to be achieving very little and the prevailing mood in the country was one of gloom, almost of despair. There was no visible improvement in the country's perennial problems. Many of the old leaders from the days of Vargas were still in the government. The cost of living continued to rise; the inflation, increasing at a rate of 30 per cent a year, was still alarming; and in the cities there were constant strikes and breakdowns in services. No one knew quite what might happen next—

although everyone, of course, had theories.

Ex-President Quadros would not be eligible to run for the presidency again until 1970, but he would be able to run for other offices. He still had great popular appeal as a "common man" who showed he knew how to speak to common men: not as a demagogue but as a man with a reputation for honesty who did not make false promises. He had never been one of the inside circle or "family" of powerful figures who reappear over and over in Brazilian politics and of whom the country's growing voting population is suspicious. Goulart was an uncertain quantity, and he seemed to be

145

restive under *parliamentarismo*. The most dangerous feature of the scene was that the newly imposed political system might prove unworkable, and that this might enable a small group of determined people to take over and have things their own way. Meanwhile the rest of the world looked on anxiously, well aware that any profound shift in Brazil's political make-up would have far-reaching repercussions throughout Central and South America.

THERE were other dilemmas. Brasília has been criticized as practically nonworkable and a drain on the country, but it keeps on working—and keeps on being a drain. The old capital of Rio, because of its tremendous population increase, is in an almost desperate condition; many years and much money will be required to provide it with an adequate water supply, as well as to iron out its transportation and communication problems. The *favela* situation grows worse—and of course it is not confined to Rio alone. Recife has a slum problem almost as bad as Rio's, as have all the larger cities. Brasília accommodates the thousands of workers it has attracted by housing them in a huge shantytown. The poverty of the agricultural workers in the northeast continues to get worse.

Beyond the problems of city and state government, Brazil is still undecided about what to do about the "hollow frontier"—the endless empty spaces that remain in the middle of the country, the "hollows" between the coastal cities and the very few cities of the interior that have never been filled in, or have been left empty as the pioneers pushed through and then beyond them. Brasília is supposed to represent a bold new push toward settling the interior, and there are faint indications that it has had some effect: small villages have grown up along the new roads that lead to it from the east and the north. The new roads constitute a formidable achievement; the one that cuts through the jungles from Belém in the north goes through jungles so dense that travelers call it "Jaguar's Promenade." But some of the

roads are in bad shape already. The one from Rio to Brasília has already been the scene of numerous washouts and other disruptions.

Brazil's troubles, almost without exception, seem to have been caused by many years of neglect on the part of inefficient governments. Of course, the Brazilian constantly blames himself and his countrymen for expecting too much from the government and for trusting that the government will take care of problems that might better be handled in other ways.

Any judgment of a country, however, must take into account a number of qualities that are in the country's favor. In Brazil's case they are qualities which will undoubtedly help guide the country through any crisis that lies ahead. For example, the Brazilian people have a genius for what is called human relations. Any social and racial tensions left over from the days of slavery are being solved more gracefully, and with less suffering, in Brazil than in any other part of the world today. The country is coping with its Indian problem as well as, if not better than, any other country with a similar problem of aboriginal inhabitants. Other countries that are not endowed with the free, simple attitude toward other races and cultures that the Brazilians have had for so long, nor with the innate Brazilian respect for other peoples, may never be able to solve their racial problems in the Brazilian way. But the Brazilian record is worth serious contemplation and the highest admiration.

THE lack of aggressiveness of the Brazilians, their willingness to compromise, to live and let live, love and let love, and their acute sense of the ridiculous and pretentious in public and private life—all are qualities the world could use more of. Their enjoyment of life has not yet been spoiled by the craze for making money; they have not yet come to the point where they automatically equate so much work with so much pay. Although this kind of reckoning may come as the inevitable price of further industrialization, perhaps the Brazilians will somehow be able to make it less harsh and competitive than it has become in the more highly developed capitalistic nations.

Brazil is in many respects a country of moderation. Extremism is looked down on. There is no death penalty. Brazil has no real enemies and has never conducted a large-scale war of conquest. Although the army has helped put an occasional president in or out of power, Brazil has never had a military dictatorship, nor does the military show signs of craving one—and this was clearly demonstrated again in the governmental crisis following the resignation of President Quadros.

THIS sense of moderation has benefited the country socially, too. Even though there is no sizable middle class—usually a prerequisite to national stability—and though the country has been divided between the very few rich and the many poor for so long, the way of life seems more democratic than that of many other countries. There is little or no awareness of all the insidious degrees of class feeling that humanity is capable of. It is still perfectly possible for an enterprising young man or woman in the professions or arts to move from one extreme of society to the other without self-consciousness or condescension on the part of anyone.

The *Integralistas,* the country's one pseudo-Fascist party, existed only briefly more than 20 years ago, and the Communist party was made illegal in 1947. Brazil has both Communists and extreme nationalists today, both representing uncertain political possibilities. The exact number of hard-core Communists in Brazil is not publicly known, although in 1958 the U.S. government estimated it at 50,000. In the cities there are groups of Communist-inspired and Communist-led students, and there are Communists or Communist followers among the army officers. But it is hard to say how serious a threat any of these represent. Certainly the widespread poverty in many areas provides a fertile ground in which Communists can operate. In many cases their professed communism seems more like a political opportunism that in a crisis might easily turn in either direction,

left or right, whichever seemed to promise the biggest personal power or gain.

The same thing is true of the extreme nationalists—those whose xenophobia can only prevent Brazil from undergoing the economic and political development which it should. The antiforeign nationalist is almost always one of two types. The first type comes usually from the newly rich class and is generally a first- or second-generation immigrant. (Most of the big new fortunes in the country have been made by immigrants.) His business has probably been granted government privileges and strong government protection. Naturally he is afraid of foreign competition, particularly of American large-scale competition, and particularly if he is an inefficient producer, or if his profits are out of proportion.

The other type of antiforeign nationalist is —and this is of course true everywhere—the man who feels he must blame all the country's troubles on some other nation. Such men can easily stir up anti-U.S. feeling among the poor and ignorant. But since the United States actually means very little to the ignorant and poor in Brazil—that is to most of the people— the blame for all ills is more often put on a local politician or simply on the government.

IT is hard, perhaps impossible, for rich nations to understand poor ones, and this is something that North Americans, with all their good intentions, often fail to realize. National poverty can produce the same symptoms and reactions everywhere—in Sicily or India, for example, as well as in Brazil. Anything a foreigner questions in Brazil—from inefficiency to dirt, from unpainted public buildings to rude bus drivers, from bad transportation to the water shortage—he is likely to blame on "the national character," or on the government's lack of concern for the people's welfare. But before he does so, he should first ask himself, Can this be explained simply by poverty? Nine times out of 10 it can.

To alleviate the ills besetting it and to enable it to maintain its economic growth, Brazil needs financial aid. But that is not all it needs. As Eugênio Gudin, one of the country's most highly respected economists and Finance Minister under President Café Filho, wrote in *O Globo*, Rio's influential afternoon paper: "The principal cause of Brazil's economic underdevelopment resides in the great scarcity, on all levels, of men prepared for the task of increasing national productivity, from engineers, entrepreneurs and administrators of high caliber to skilled workmen. Our chief goal, therefore, should be the formation of a nucleus of educated men. For this we need . . . to import hundreds of technicians and teachers and to send thousands of students to foreign countries, not only in the fields of the sciences but especially in the various branches of engineering and industrial techniques."

Gudin blames the present inflation and dangerous state of affairs in great part on the building of Brasília and on the government waste of the Kubitschek era. The most important task confronting Brazil, he feels, is the elimination of the waste and misuse of the nation's resources. But beyond that, special efforts should also be made to encourage assistance, public and private, both to the creation of an "educated nucleus" and to the developments that will actually increase the country's income and satisfy the urgent needs of the people.

FOR what Brazil lacks above all else is a good, sound government, and this can be achieved only by raising the level of society as a whole through education and through increased material well-being. If that can be done, there would be no problem in Brazil that good government could not resolve, because the government would then be a reflection of a healthy body politic. Under good administration, industrial and material progress would undoubtedly take place at a tremendous rate—because so many of the other essentials are there.

Even without good government, of course, Brazil has achieved a great deal. "Progress" does not always coincide with "civilization," and many countries have maintained high standards of artistic and social performance without the benefits of good government. Brazil has an impressive body of sophisticated arts and letters and a thriving folk culture. It has many qualities of character and society that go only with high civilization. One should not make exaggerated cultural or social claims for Brazil; still, politics aside, it has done remarkably well.

Obviously, barring some world-wide disaster, Brazil is going to push and be pushed into industrialization. There is no doubt that it will one day be a major world power; the question is, what kind of men will be running the country then, and what kind of a country will it be? Can Brazil in effect beat the clock—will social and political reforms be put through quickly enough, and economic improvements introduced effectively enough, or will the people's demands for a better life bring about a social revolution? For the time being, however, it is still one country where human man is still considered more important than producing man, or consuming man, or political man.

EVERYONE who visits Brazil agrees that the ordinary, average Brazilians are a wonderful people, cheerful, sweet-tempered, witty and patient—incredibly patient. To see them standing in line for hours, literally for hours, in lines folded back on themselves two or three times the length of a city block, only to get aboard a broken-down, recklessly driven bus and return to their tiny suburban houses, where like as not these days the street has not been repaired, nor the garbage collected, and there may even be no water—to see this is to marvel at their patience. Other people undergoing the same trials would surely stage a revolution every month or so. There may still be more than one *golpe*, or coup, in the offing to change the course of government—because there is certainly a growing determination among Brazilians to achieve a better government. But if this determination brings troubles, let us hope they can be solved with the usual Brazilian moderation. Brazilians have never had the government they should have; there is no knowing how long it will be before they get it.

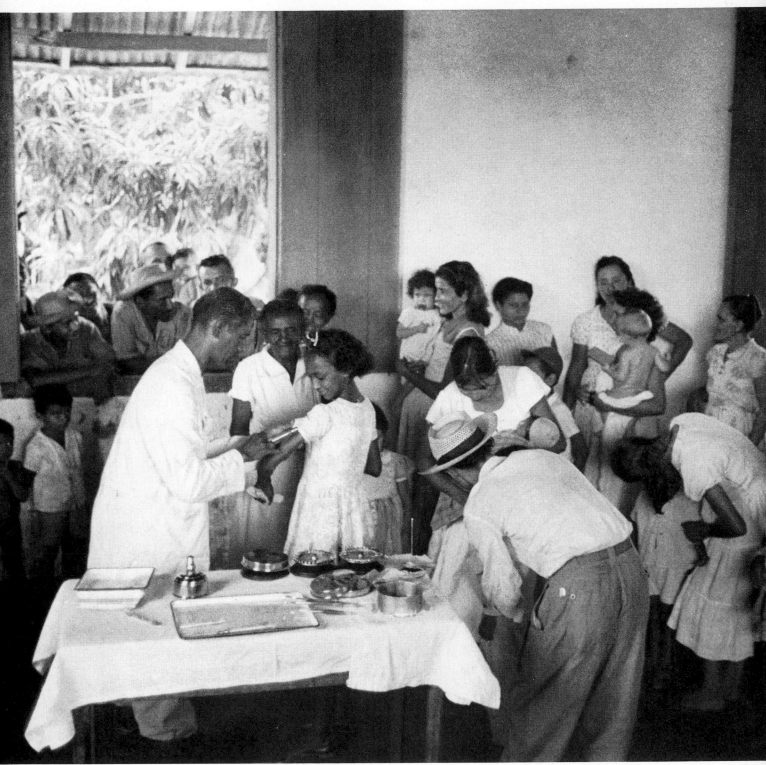

In the Mato Grosso, Indians receive inoculations at a rural clinic. Next page: Voters register at a Rio de Janeiro polling station.

A FUTURE POWER, Brazil must strengthen its society by humane reforms . . .

. . . in order to create the vigorous and informed citizenry it requires to establish an

effective government and to reap lasting benefits from its great store of natural wealth

Appendix

HISTORICAL DATES

Pre-1500   Primitive Indian tribes settle in the area which is now Brazil. By 1500 they number about a million persons. The coastal Tupi, an agricultural and fishing people, are the tribesmen who later have most contact with Europeans and become their first slaves

1500   Pedro Alvares Cabral, an explorer ostensibly on his way to India, lands in Brazil and claims it for the Portuguese crown

1501-c.1530   Portuguese traders explore Brazilian coast and bargain with the Indians for brazilwood, used in making dyes. Portugal, primarily interested in trade with the Far East, makes little effort to develop Brazil

1516   France threatens Portuguese brazilwood trade. Portuguese ships are ordered to sink all French vessels found in Brazilian waters

1532   Under the leadership of Martim Afonso de Souza, settlers found Brazil's first permanent colony, São Vicente, near Santos. Sugar cane, first planted in São Vicente, becomes basis of Brazil's early economy

1534   To encourage colonization and exploitation of the new territories, King João III of Portugal apportions Brazil among 12 nobles, each of whom is responsible for development of his fief or captaincy. The experiment is only a partial success; most of the grantees fail to obtain sufficient colonists

1538   First full shipment of Negro slaves arrives in Brazil from West Africa. In subsequent centuries at least three million Negro slaves are brought to Brazil

1549   Portugal evolves a new plan providing for a central administration in Brazil to bring the colony under more efficient control

1553   Jesuits found an Indian mission which becomes São Paulo

1555   Under Nicolas de Villegaignon, the French again menace Portuguese conquests, take possession of the harbor of Rio de Janeiro

1560   Portuguese force surrender of the French garrison

1567   To ward off French encroachment, the Portuguese found a settlement at Rio de Janeiro

1580   Portuguese and Spanish crowns are united under Philip II of Spain

c. 1600   Gold-seeking *bandeirantes* begin century-long series of expeditions into the interior. They take Indian slaves and vastly extend Brazil's frontiers

1624-1625   Dutch threaten Portuguese possession of Brazil, briefly capture city of Bahia (Salvador)

1630-1632   Dutch capture Recife and Olinda, key cities in the sugar-producing region of Pernambuco. The region thrives and the Dutch extend their rule south and north along the coast

1633-1695   Escaped Negro slaves form the Confederacy of Palmares in the forests of Pernambuco. Ruled by its own king, the community swells to about 20,000 members, is finally destroyed by Portuguese armed forces

1640   Dom João IV is crowned King of Portugal. The union of Spain and Portugal ends

1641   Brazilian colonists launch uprisings against the Dutch

1654   With scant support from Portugal, Brazilians drive the Dutch out of their last strongholds

1693-1728   Gold and diamonds discovered in Minas Gerais, Mato Grosso and Goiás. Towns spring up in hitherto unbroken wilderness

1789-1792   Conspiracy for independence led by Joaquim José da Silva Xavier, or "Tiradentes" (Toothpuller), a part-time dentist, ends in failure. Tiradentes killed

1808   Forced into exile by Napoleon, Portugal's royal family and thousands of Portuguese aristocrats come to Brazil. The Prince Regent (afterward King João VI of Portugal) opens the ports of Brazil to all friendly nations, ending Portuguese trade monopoly

1815   Brazil decreed integral part of monarchy, equal in status to Portugal

1817   Popular revolt against monarchy breaks out in Pernambuco and a short-lived republic is formed

1821   João VI returns to Portugal, appointing his son Dom Pedro as regent in Brazil. Portugal attempts to restore Brazil to former dependency and orders Dom Pedro to return home

1822   Dom Pedro, supported by majority of Brazilians, refuses to return to Portugal, convokes a legislative and constituent assembly and proclaims the independence of Brazil. He is crowned emperor of the country

1824   A liberal constitution is adopted. Pedro I agrees to rule

1831   Dom Pedro I abdicates in favor of his five-year-old son, Pedro II

1831-1840   Regency rule: civil war in the provinces and insubordination in the army

1840-1889   Reign of Dom Pedro II, marked by enlightened social and administrative reforms

1850   Laws against further importation of slaves enforced for the first time

1864-1870   Combined forces of Brazil, Argentina and Uruguay fight and win costly war against Paraguay

1871   Bill providing for gradual and partial emancipation of slaves passed by Parliament

1888   Complete emancipation of slaves decreed

1889   Benjamin Constant Botelho de Magalhães and Manuel Deodoro da Fonseca force abdication of Pedro II and proclaim a republic. Deodoro da Fonseca becomes head of provisional government

1891   Government adopts new constitution, under which Deodoro da Fonseca becomes first president. Shortly afterwards he assumes dictatorial powers and is forced to resign

1894   First civilian president, Prudente José de Moraes Barros, is elected

1917   Brazil declares war on Germany

1929   World economic upheaval causes a collapse of the coffee market. Brazil plagued by financial and political disorders

1930   Getúlio Vargas, defeated candidate for presidency, charges the election was fraudulent, leads successful revolt and seizes the presidency

1932   Revolt in São Paulo

1934   New constitution, forbidding the re-election of president for successive terms, is promulgated. Vargas legally elected president

1937   Vargas suspends forthcoming presidential election

1938   Last major revolt against Vargas, who rules as dictator until 1945

1942   World War II: Brazil declares war on Italy and Germany

1945   Bloodless military coup overthrows Vargas. General Eurico Gaspar Dutra elected president

1946   New constitution promulgated

1950   Vargas re-elected president

1954   Pressured to resign, Vargas commits suicide

1955-1960   Juscelino Kubitschek presidency. Capital moved inland to Brasília

1960   Jânio Quadros elected president, João Goulart vice-president

1961   Quadros resigns, creating constitutional crisis. Goulart becomes president with reduced powers

FOR FURTHER READING

CHAPTER 1: THE BRAZILIAN PEOPLE

Freyre, Gilberto, *Brazil, An Interpretation*. Alfred A. Knopf, 1947.

Livermore, H. V., ed., *Portugal and Brazil, An Introduction*. Oxford University Press, 1953.

Portrait of a Great Country, Brazil. Colibris Editora, Rio de Janeiro, 1959.

Schurz, William Lytle, *Brazil, the Infinite Country*. E. P. Dutton, 1961. *This New World*. E. P. Dutton, 1954.

Smith, T. Lynn and Alexander Marchant, eds., *Brazil*. The Dryden Press, 1951.

Zweig, Stefan, *Brazil, Land of the Future*. The Viking Press, 1941.

CHAPTER 2: GEOGRAPHY AND EARLY HISTORY

Agassiz, Louis, *A Journey in Brazil*. Houghton Mifflin, 1896.

Bates, Henry Walter, *The Naturalist on the Amazon*. E. P. Dutton, 1910.

Burton, Sir Richard, *Explorations of the Highlands of the Brazil*. Tinsley Brothers, London, 1869.

Carlson, Fred A., *Geography of Latin America*. Prentice-Hall, 1943.

Cruls, Gastão, *Hiléia Amazonica*. José Olympio, Rio de Janeiro, 1958.

Darwin, Charles, *The Voyage of the Beagle*. J. M. Dent and Sons, London, 1906.

Greenlee, William Brooks, ed., *Cabral's Voyage to Brazil and India*. Hakluyt Society, 1938.

Guenther, Konrad, *A Naturalist in Brazil*. Houghton Mifflin, 1931.

James, Preston E., *Latin America*. The Odyssey Press, 1959.

Lévi-Strauss, Claude, *Tristes Tropiques*. Criterion Books, 1961.

Matthews, Kenneth, *Brazilian Interior*. P. Davies, London, 1956.

Tomlinson, H. M., *The Sea and The Jungle*. The Modern Library, 1928.

CHAPTER 3: THE NINETEENTH CENTURY

Calogeras, João Pandiá, *A History of Brazil*. University of North Carolina Press, 1939.

Crow, John A., *The Epic of Latin America*. Doubleday, 1946.

Da Costa, Sérgio Corrêa, *Every Inch a King, A Biography of Dom Pedro I, First Emperor of Brazil*. Macmillan, 1950.

Freyre, Gilberto, *The Masters and the Slaves; a Study in the Development of Brazilian Civilization*. Alfred A. Knopf, 1946.

Haring, C. H., *Empire in Brazil*. Harvard University Press, 1958.

Herring, Hubert, *A History of Latin America*. Alfred A. Knopf, 1961.

Martin, Michael Rheta, and Gabriel H. Lovett, *An Encyclopedia of Latin-American History*. Abelard-Schuman, 1956.

Peck, Anne Merriman, *The Pageant of South American History*. Longmans, Green, 1941.

Pombo, Rocha, *História do Brasil*. W. M. Jackson, Rio de Janeiro, 1953.

Rippy, J. Fred, *Latin America, A Modern History*. University of Michigan Press, 1958.

Sousa, Octavio Tarquinio de, *A Vida de D. Pedro I*. 3 vols. José Olympio, Rio de Janeiro, 1952.

Sousa, Octavio Tarquinio de, and Sérgio Buarque de Holanda, *História do Brasil*. José Olympio, Rio de Janeiro, 1944.

Thomas, Alfred Barnaby, *Latin America, A History*. Macmillan, 1956.

Williams, Mary Wilhelmine, *Dom Pedro the Magnanimous, Second Emperor of Brazil*. University of North Carolina Press, 1937.

Worcester, Donald E., and Wendell G. Schaeffer, *The Growth and Culture of Latin America*. Oxford University Press, 1956.

CHAPTER 4: THREE CAPITALS

Harding, Bertita, *Southern Empire, Brazil*. Coward-McCann, 1948.

Kelsey, Vera, *Brazil in Capitals*. Harper and Brothers, 1942.

Maurois, André, *Rio de Janeiro*. F. Nathan, Paris, 1953.

Morse, Richard M., *From Community to Metropolis; A Biography of São Paulo, Brazil*. University of Florida Press, 1958.

Nagel Travel Guide Series, *Brazil*. Nagel Publishers, 1955.

New World Guides to the Latin American Republics, Vol. 3. Duell, Sloan and Pearce, 1950.

São Paulo, Fastest-Growing City in the World. Livraria Kosmos Editora, Rio de Janeiro, 1954.

Violich, Francis, *Cities of Latin America; Housing and Planning to the South*. Reinhold Publishing, 1944.

CHAPTER 5: ECONOMICS

Hunnicutt, Benjamin H., *Brazil, World Frontier*. D. Van Nostrand, 1949.

Jobim, José, *Brazil in the Making*. Macmillan, 1943.

Kuznets, Simon and others, *Economic Growth: Brazil, India, Japan*. Duke University Press, 1955.

Loeb, G. F., *Industrialization and Balanced Growth with Special Reference to Brazil*. Gregory Lounz, 1958.

Normano, J. F., *Brazil: A Study of Economic Types*. University of North Carolina Press, 1935.

Stein, Stanley J., *Vassouras, A Brazilian Coffee Country, 1850-1900*. Harvard University Press, 1957.

Survey of the Brazilian Economy, 1960. Brazilian Embassy, Washington, D.C., 1960.

Wythe, George, *Industry in Latin America*. Columbia University Press, 1949.

CHAPTERS 6 & 7: THE ARTS

Apel, Paul H., *Music of the Americas North and South*. Vantage Press, 1958.

Atlantic Monthly, *Perspective of Brazil*. Intercultural Publications, 1956.

Bandeira, Manuel, *Noções de História das Literaturas*. Companhia Editora Nacional, São Paulo, 1942.

Bazin, Germain, *L'Architecture Religieuse Baroque au Brésil*. 2 vols. Museum of Art, São Paulo, 1956-1958.

Crawford, William Rex, *A Century of Latin-American Thought*. Harvard University Press, 1944.

Ellison, Fred P., *Brazil's New Novel; Four Northeastern Masters*. University of California Press, 1954.

Fitts, Dudley, ed., *Anthology of Contemporary Latin American Poetry*. New Directions, 1942.

Goodwin, Philip L., *Brazil Builds; Architecture New and Old, 1652-1942*. The Museum of Modern Art, New York, 1943.

Hitchcock, Henry-Russell, *Latin American Architecture Since 1945*. The Museum of Modern Art, New York, 1955.

Kubler, George and Martin Soria, *Art and Architecture in Spain and Portugal and their American Dominions*. Penguin Books, 1959.

Machado de Assis, Joaquim Maria, *Dom Casmurro*, trans. by William L. Grossman. Noonday Press, 1953. *Epitaph of a Small Winner*, trans. by Helen Caldwell. Noonday Press, 1952. *Philosopher or Dog?* trans. by Clotilde Wilson. Noonday Press, 1954.

Mindlin, Henrique E., *Modern Architecture in Brazil*. Colibris Editora, Rio de Janeiro, 1956.

Onís, Harriet de, *The Golden Land, An Anthology of Latin American Folklore in Literature*. Alfred A. Knopf, 1948.

Pierson, Donald, *Survey of Literature on Brazil of Sociological Significance Published up to 1940*. Harvard University Press, 1945.

Putnam, Samuel, *Marvelous Journey, A Survey of Four Centuries of Brazilian Writing*. Alfred A. Knopf, 1948.

Verissimo, Erico, *Brazilian Literature; An Outline*. Macmillan, 1945.

CHAPTER 8: INDIVIDUALS AND GROUPS

Brant, Alice, *The Diary of "Helena Morley,"* trans. by Elizabeth Bishop. Farrar, Straus and Cudahy, 1957.

Callcott, Maria Graham, *Journal of a*

Voyage to Brazil and Residence there During Part of the Years 1821, 1822, 1823. Longman, Hurst, etc., London, 1824.

Fleming, Peter, *Brazilian Adventure.* Charles Scribner's Sons, 1933.

Harris, Marvin, *Town and Country in Brazil.* Columbia University Press, 1956.

Pierson, Donald, *Negroes in Brazil.* University of Chicago Press, 1942.

Radin, Paul, *Indians of South America.* Doubleday, Doran, 1942.

Ramos, Arthur, *The Negro in Brazil.* Associated Publishers, 1939.

Roosevelt, Theodore, *Through the Brazilian Wilderness.* Charles Scribner's Sons, 1914.

Sick, Helmut, *Tukani.* Taplinger, 1959.

Smith, T. Lynn, *Brazil, People and Insti-tutions.* Louisiana State University Press, 1954.

Steward, Julian H., *Handbook of South American Indians,* Vol. 3, *The Tropical Forest Tribes.* United States Government Printing Office, Washington, D.C., 1948.

Wagley, Charles, *Amazon Town, A Study of Man in the Tropics.* Macmillan, 1953. *Race and Class in Rural Brazil.* UNESCO, 1952.

Chapters 9 & 10: Recent Politics

Camacho, J. A., *Brazil, An Interim Assessment.* Royal Institute of International Affairs, London, 1951.

Da Cunha, Euclides, *Rebellion in the Backlands,* trans. by Samuel Putnam. University of Chicago Press, 1944.

Fitzgibbon, Russell H., ed., *The Constitutions of the Americas.* University of Chicago Press, 1948.

Graham, Robert Bonfine Cunninghame, *A Brazilian Mystic.* W. Heinemann, London, 1920.

Loewenstein, Karl, *Brazil under Vargas.* Macmillan, 1942.

MacDonald, Austin F., *Latin American Government and Politics.* Thomas Y. Crowell, 1954.

Phillips, Henry Albert, *Brazil, Bulwark of Inter-American Relations.* Hastings House, 1945.

Pike, Frederick B., ed., *Freedom and Reform in Latin America.* University of Notre Dame Press, 1959.

Szulc, Tad, *Twilight of the Tyrants.* Holt, Rinehart, Winston, 1959.

FAMOUS BRAZILIAN CULTURAL FIGURES AND THEIR PRINCIPAL WORKS

ARCHITECTURE AND SCULPTURE

Lisbôa, Antônio Francisco (Aleijadinho)	1738-1814	Architect and sculptor: design and decoration of church of São Francisco at Ouro Prêto, statues of the 12 prophets at church of the Bom Jesus de Matosinhos at Congonhas do Campo
Fonseca e Silva, Valentim da (Mestre Valentim)	-1813	Secular sculptural groups and elaborate fountains; religious sculptures and church decorations
Grandjean de Montigny, Auguste-Henri	1776-1850	Member of French artistic mission invited to Brazil in 1816 to found a Brazilian academy of fine arts. Designed official buildings in Rio de Janeiro, including the headquarters of the academy
Martins, Maria	1900-	Large energetic sculptures: *Impossible, St. Francis of Assisi*
Costa, Lúcio	1902-	Supervision of restoration of historic towns; apartment buildings, Rio de Janeiro; private residences; city-planner of the new capital of Brazil, Brasília
Moreira, Jorge Machado	1904-	Ministry of Education and Health building, Rio de Janeiro (with others); architect of University City of Brazil, Rio de Janeiro
Niemeyer Soares Filho, Oscar	1907-	Ministry of Education and Health building, Rio de Janeiro (with others); Brazilian pavilion, New York World's Fair, 1939; modern churches, private residences; exhibition centers; architect of the government buildings in Brasília
Burle Marx, Roberto	1909-	Painter and landscape architect. Gardens: Santos Dumont airport, Rio de Janeiro; Ministry of Education and Health building, Rio de Janeiro; Museum of Modern Art, Rio de Janeiro; private residences in Brazil; public park in Venezuela
Reidy, Affonso Eduardo	1909-	Ministry of Education and Health building, Rio de Janeiro (with others); Pedregulho housing development, Rio de Janeiro; Paraguay-Brazil Experimental School in Paraguay; Museum of Modern Art, Rio de Janeiro
Mindlin, Henrique Ephim	1911-	Tres Leões apartment building, São Paulo; private residences, São Paulo and Rio de Janeiro; offices and synagogues
Bernardes, Sergio Wladimir	1919-	Private residences and apartment buildings; exhibition buildings; clubs

ART

Post, Frans	c.1612-1680	Lived in Pernambuco during the Dutch occupation. Paintings of the plants, animals, dwellings and plantations of early northeast Brazil: *View of Pernambuco*
Almeida Junior, José Ferraz de	1850-1899	Intimate scenes of provincial life of São Paulo: *Nhá Chica, The Guitar Player*
Segall, Lasar	1890-	Expressionist. *Eternos Caminhantes, Pogrom, Navio de Emigrantes, Guerra*
Guignard, Alberto da Veiga	1896-	Imagist. *Stations of the Cross, Ouro Prêto, St. John's Eve*
Cavalcanti, Emiliano di	1897-	Paintings, murals and posters depicting people and landscapes of Brazil
Amaral, Tarsila do	c.1899-	One of the founders of Brazilian modernist movement in painting. *The Negress, The Cannibal*
Portinari, Cândido	1903-	Murals and paintings depicting people and life of Brazil. Murals: Ministry of Education and Health, Rio de Janeiro; Brazilian pavilion at 1939 World's Fair, New York; Hispanic Foundation, Library of Congress, Washington, D.C.; United Nations building, New York
Camargo, Iberê	1914-	Abstractionist whose anatomic approach has surrealistic overtones
Dacosta, Milton	1915-	Abstractionist who uses geometric decompositions of shapes and distinct coloring

Ostrower, Fayga	1920-	Engraver with delicate and highly personal abstract style
De Lamonica, Roberto	1923-	Engraver who gains lyrical spatial effects through imaginative use of line and flat areas
Serpa, Ivan	1923-	Abstractionist whose style of painting and collage has evolved through analytical cubism
Mabe, Manabu	1924-	Japanese-born abstractionist who uses symbols resembling oriental calligraphy
Magalhães, Aloisio Sergio	1927-	Painter and engraver who brings vivid color to his abstractions. Developer of avant-garde printing techniques
Bonomi, Maria	1935-	Engraver who uses dynamic counterpoint of bold black and white forms; occasionally employs color

MUSIC

Nunes Garcia, Father José Maurício	1767-1830	Religious music: *Missa de Requiem, Missa de Santa Cecilia*
Gomez, Carlos	1836-1896	Opera: *Il Guarany, Lo Schiavo*
Nepomuceno, Alberto	1864-1920	Orchestral music with Brazilian folk themes: *Serie Brasileira.* Piano music, songs
Villa-Lobos, Heitor	1884-1959	Synthesis of Brazilian folk rhythms and Bach's contrapuntal technique: *Bachianas Brasileiras.* Orchestral music, operas, songs
Fernandes, Oscar Lorenzo	1897-1948	Opera: *Malazarte*
Mignone, Francisco	1897-	Opera: *Contratador de Diamantes*
Guarnieri, Camargo	1907-	Orchestral music: *Suite Vila Rica.* Choral works, chamber music

LITERATURE

Matos, Gregório de	c.1623-1696	Poetry: *Obras poéticas*
Silva, Antônio José da (O Judeu)	1705-1739	Plays: *Guerras do Alecrim e Mangerona*
Costa, Cláudio Manoel da	1729-1789	Poetry: *Obras poéticas, Vila Rica*
Gonzaga, Tomás Antônio	1744-1809	Poetry: *Marília de Dirceu*
Lisboa, João Francisco	1812-1863	History: *Jornal de Timon*
Martins Pena, Luís Carlos (Theater)	1815-1848	Plays: *O Juiz de paz na roça, O Judas em sábado de aleluia, O Noviço*
Varnhagen, Francisco Adolfo de	1816-1878	History: *História geral do Brasil*
Macedo, Joaquim Manuel de	1820-1882	Novels: *A Moreninha, O moço louro, Rosa*
Gonçalves Dias, Antônio	1823-1864	Poetry: *Primeiros cantos, Segundos cantos e Sextilhas de frei Antão, Últimos cantos, Os Timbiras*
Alencar, José Martiniano de	1829-1877	Novels: *O Guaraní, Iracema, Senhora, O Sertaneio*
Almeida, Manuel Antônio de	1831-1855	Novel: *Memórias de um sargento de milícias*
Machado de Assis, Joaquim Maria	1839-1908	Novels: *Memórias póstumas de Braz Cubas, Quincas Borba, Dom Casmurro, Memorial de Aires*
Castro Alves, Antônio de	1847-1871	Poetry: *Espumas flutuantes, Vozes d'Africa, Os Escravos*
Nabuco, Joaquim	1849-1910	History and reminiscences: *Um estadista do Império, Minha formação*
Romero, Sílvio	1851-1914	Folklore and literary criticism: *Contos populares do Brasil, História da literatura brasileira*
Abreu, João Capistrano de	1853-1927	History: *O descobrimento do Brasil e seu desenvolvimento no século, Capítulos da história colonial*
Azevedo, Aluízio de	1857-1913	Novels: *O Mulato, Casa de pensão*
Correia, Raimundo	1860-1911	Poetry: *Versos e versões*
Coelho Neto, Henrique	1864-1934	Novels: *Sertão, A Tormenta, Rei Negro*
Bilac, Olavo	1865-1918	Poetry: *Poesias*
Cunha, Euclides da	1866-1909	Sociology: *Os Sertões*
Lima Barreto, Afonso Henriques de	1881-1922	Novels: *Recordações do escrivão Isaías Caminha, O triste fim de Polycarpo Quaresma*
Monteiro Lobato, José Bento	1882-1948	Tales: *Urupés*
Bandeira, Manuel	1886-	Poetry: *Poesias completas*
Almeida, José Américo de	1887-	Novel: *A Bagaceira*
Amado, Gilberto	1887-	Essays and reminiscences: *A dança sôbre o abismo, História da minha infância*
Ramos, Graciliano	1892-1953	Novels: *Angústia, Vidas Sêcas*
Andrade, Mário de	1893-1945	Novels, poetry and essays: *Macunaíma, Ensaio sôbre música brasileira*
Ataíde, Tristão de	1893-	Literary criticism: *Estudos, Poesia brasileira contemporânea*
Lima, Jorge de	1895-1953	Poetry: *Invenção de Orfeu*
Freyre, Gilberto	1900-	Sociology: *Casa Grande & Senzala*
Lins do Rêgo, José	1901-1957	Novels: *Menino de engenho, Fogo morto, Os cangaceiros*
Meireles, Cecília	1901-	Poetry: *Mar absoluto*
Drummond de Andrade, Carlos	1902-	Poetry: *Fazendeiro do ar & Poesia até agora*
Calmon, Pedro	1905-	History: *História do Brasil*
Veríssimo, Erico	1905-	Novel: *O Tempo e o vento*
Faria, Otávio de	1908-	Novels: *Mundos mortos, Retrato da morte*
Guimarães Rosa, João	1910-	Novel and tales: *Grande sertão veredas*
Queiroz, Rachel de	1910-	Novels: *O Quinze, As três Marias, João Miguel, Caminho de pedras*
Amado, Jorge	1912-	Novels: *Jubiabá, Gabriela, Cravo e Canela*
Rodrigues, Nelson	1912-	Plays: *Vestido de noiva, Boca de Ouro*
Cabral de Mello Neto, João	1920-	Poetry: *Cão sem plumas, Duas aquas*
Lispector, Clarice	1920-	Novel: *Maçã no escuro*
Suassuna, Ariano	1927-	Plays: *Auto da compadecida*

Credits

The sources for the illustrations in this book are shown below. Credits for pictures from left to right are separated by commas, top to bottom by dashes.

Cover—Dmitri Kessel

8, 9—Lisl Steiner

16—Paulo Muniz

17—Michael Teague

18—Frank J. Scherschel for LIFE EN ESPAÑOL

19—David Drew Zingg—David Vestal

20, 21—Photo Researchers, Inc., Dmitri Kessel

22, 23, 24—Dmitri Kessel

27—Courtesy American Geographical Society drawn after original by M. M. Malatesta, Zattera and Antilli

32—David Drew Zingg

33—Dmitri Kessel

34, 35—Dmitri Kessel, Frank J. Scherschel for LIFE EN ESPAÑOL

36—Anthony Linck

37—Pix

38, 39—E.A.Gourley

40, 41—Francisco Marques dos Santos

45—The Bettmann Archive

47—Paulo Muniz

48—Leonard McCombe

49—Paulo Muniz for LIFE EN ESPAÑOL

50, 51—Paulo Muniz for LIFE EN ESPAÑOL, Photo Researchers, Inc.

52, 53—Dmitri Kessel

57—Map by Matt Greene

59—Paulo Muniz for LIFE EN ESPAÑOL

60—Rene Burri from Magnum

61 through 68—Dmitri Kessel

73—Map by Fred Eng

76—John and Bini Moss from Photo Researchers, Inc.

77 through 80—Dmitri Kessel

81—Peter Anderson from Black Star for LIFE EN ESPAÑOL

82, 83—Elliott Erwitt from Magnum

89—Lisl Steiner

90—David Drew Zingg for LIFE EN ESPAÑOL

91—Marc and Evelyne Bernheim from Photo Researchers, Inc.

92, 93—Marcel Gautherot

94, 95—Brassai from Rapho-Guillumette, Leonard McCombe

96—Michael Teague

102—Woodcut by Maria Bonomi courtesy Roland de Aenlle Gallery

105—Photo Researchers, Inc.

106—Paulo Muniz—Photo Researchers, Inc.

107—Paulo Muniz for LIFE EN ESPAÑOL

108—Dmitri Kessel

109—© Rollie McKenna, Paulo Muniz

110, 111—Claudia Andujar

112, 113—Radio Times Hulton Picture Library

118, 119—Rene Burri from Magnum

120, 121—Paulo Muniz

122, 123—Brassai from Rapho-Guillumette, Paulo Muniz

124—Paulo Muniz for LIFE EN ESPAÑOL

125—Paulo Muniz

126—Hart Preston

134, 135—Agencia Nacional, Manchete

136, 137—Andrew St. George

138, 139—Paulo Muniz except center Frank J. Scherschel for LIFE EN ESPAÑOL

140, 141—Gordon Parks

142, 143—Andrew St. George

144—Dmitri Kessel

149—Rene Burri from Magnum

150, 151—Paulo Muniz

ACKNOWLEDGMENTS

The editors of this book received valuable assistance from Marcos C. de Azambuja, Adviser to the Brazilian Mission to the United Nations, and from Ariane Brunel, Editorial Assistant and Adviser to *The Columbia Encyclopedia*, both of whom read and commented on portions of the text. Miss Bishop is indebted for advice and assistance to Lota de Macedo Soares, Rodrigo Mello Franco de Andrade, Eugênio Gudin, Rosalina Azevedo Leão, Dario de Almeida Magalhães, Rachel de Queiroz and Maria Augusta Costa Ribeiro.

Index

* This symbol in front of a page number indicates a photograph or painting of subject mentioned.

Abreu, Casimiro de, 103
Academy of Letters, 104
Africa: Brazilian troops in, in World War II, 131; coffee rivalry of, 72; slaves from, 54
African influences, 54-55; in folk art and music, 84, 86, 101, 102; in religion, 55, 85, 89
Agriculture, 69, 72; cattle raising, 29, 70-71; cereals, 75; coffee, 70, 71-72, *76-77; fruit and vegetables, 75, 115; labor, 69, 74, 142, 146; methods, 74; need for diversification of, 72, 74; products, *map* 73; sugar, 70, 72, 74; tobacco, 75
Aid, economic: need for, 147-148; by U.S., 75, 131
Air Force, 131
Alagôas, 74
Alcoholic drinks, 14-15, 74
Aleijadinho (Antônio Francisco Lisbôa), 100, 104, 114; sculptures by, *96
Alencar, José, 102
Alliance of National Liberation, 130
Amado, Jorge, 104
Amazon basin: climate of, 28; housing in, 99; products of, 74, 75
Amazon River, *34, 57; cities on, 12, 20, 59, 74; fishing, 71; origin of name, 30; physical data, 30; shipping on, 29
Amazonas, state, 71
American Revolution, 31, 42
Andes, 28
Andrade, Mário de, 104, 114
Angola, 30
Arantes do Nascimento, Edson, *125
Araucaria, 74
Architects, 97-98, *108-109
Architecture: of Brasília, 57, *59-67, 109; churches, *17, 100, *122-123; conditions for, 98-99; contemporary, *17, *59-67, 97-98, 100, 109; destruction of old, 55, 56, 100-101; Jesuit style baroque, 100; materials, 98, 99-100; 19th Century neoclassic, 100; surviving colonial, *17, *20-21, 98, 99-100
Argentina, 15, 42, 45, 129
Aristocracy: old landed, 44, 45, 46, 50; surviving elite, *47-49, 50
Army: coups, 129, 131, 132, 147; and emancipation of slaves, 46; Communists in, 147; opposes Goulart, 133, 138; in World War II, 130-131
Art, 97-104, 148; black and white work, 101, *102; climate of, 104, 105; painting, 101, *106-

107, *110; racial tolerance in, 104, 114; respect for, 97, 104; São Paulo *Bienal*, 101, *110-111; sculpture, *64-65, *96, 100. *See also* Architecture; Folk art; Literature; Music
Atomic ores, 29, *map* 73, 75
Auiti Indians, *37
Automobile industry, 19, 132

Backlands. *See* Interior Brazil; Sertão
Backlands, Rebellion in the, da Cunha, 104
Bahia (Salvador), city, *20-21, 31, 42, *52-53, 119; churches in, 100, *123; history of, 54-55
Bahia, state, 12, 26, 53, 85; economy of, 29, 70, 72, 75; religious rebellion in, 104, 128
Balangandãs, 54, 85
Banana, 29, *map* 73, 75
Bandeirantes, 30-31, 56, 70
Bandiera, Manuel, 103
Bank of Brazil, 43
Baudelaire, Charles, 102
Behring, Edith, 101
Belém, 12, *20, 100, 146
Bernardes, Sergio, 98
Birth control, 11
Birth rate, 11
Bolivia, 129
Bonfim festival, 54
Bonifácio, José, 56-57
Bonomi, Maria, 101; block print by, *102
Braganza, House of, 41, 44, 101
Brasília, *8-9, 53, 57-58, *59-67, 98, 132, 146, 148; layout of, *map* 57, 109
Brazil: discovery of, 25; geography of, 28-29; 1502 map of, 27; origin of name, 25-26
Brazil nuts, 29, *map* 73, 74
Brazilian Wilderness, Through the, Roosevelt, 115
Bresilium, 25
Brussels World's Fair, 98
Building industry, 98
Bulhões de Carvalho da Fonseca, Thereza, *47
Bumba-meu-boi, 87, *92-93
Burle Marx, Roberto, 99, *109

Cabo Frio, 71
Caboclo, 28
Cabral, Pedro Alvares, 25-26, 28
Cabral de Mello Neto, João, 103
Cachaça, 74
Café Filho, João, 131, 148
Camargo, Iberê, 101
Camayurá Indians, *36
Caminha, Pero Vaz de, 26-28
Candomblé. *See Macumba*
Canudos, war of, 104, 128
Cape Verde Islands, 26, 70

Capital cities, 53-58. *See also* Bahia; Brasília; Rio de Janeiro
Capitalism, 45
Capoeira, 55
Captaincies, 29, 53-54
Caracas, 99
Cariocas, 12, 58
Carnauba wax, 74-75
Carnival, 11, *82-83, 87-88, *89-91
Carrancas, 86
Carvalho, Odete de, 117
Castro, Fidel, 142
Castro Alves, Antônio de, 103
Catholicism, 10, 123. *See also* Roman Catholic Church
Cattle raising, 29, 70-71, *map* 73
Cavalcanti, Emiliano di, 101
Cayapó Indians, 116
Ceará, 28, 71, 74, 84, 117
Charque, 71
Chemical industry, 72
Chesterton, G. K., 102
Children, 10-11
China, Communist, 133
Christianization, 30
Churches, *17, 100; São Francisco de Assis, *122-123
Cities, 16, 20, 59, 72; capitals, 53-58; colonial, 29, 31; of Empire period, 45; life in, *16, *18-19; migration to, 16, 56; modernization of, 128; problems of, 146; removal of old buildings in, 55, 56, 100-101; surviving old buildings in, *17, *20-21, 100
Civil rights, 114; abolition of slavery, 45-46; under Pedro II, 44; suppressed by Vargas, 132; voting, 130; of women, 117
Climate, 28
Coal resources, 29, *map* 73, 75
Coffee: areas, 71-72, *map* 73; exports, 71, 76; growing of, *76-77; importance of, in Brazilian economy, 45, 46, 70, 71-72, 76; world market, 76
Colonization, 29-31, 54, 70
Columbus, Christopher, 25, 26
Commercial Code, 45
Communications, 29, 45, 129. *See also* Transportation
Communists, 129, 130, 147
Comte, Auguste, 46
Conceição, Maria da, 9-10
Congonhas do Campo, 100
Congress: authorizes Brasília, 57; changes government system (1961), 133, 137; under the "Counselors," 129; deposed by Vargas, 130; and Quadros, 133
Congress building, *66-67
Conselheiro. *See* Maciel, Antônio
Constant Botelho de Magalhães, Benjamin, 46

Constituent Assembly of 1934, 130
Constitutions: amendment of 1961, 133, 137; Empire, 43; of 1934, 130; of 1946, 57, 114, 131; of Vargas, 130
Construction industry, 98
Convicts, Portuguese, 28
Cooking, 15, 54
Copacabana, *22-23, 55, 99; Eighteen of, 129, 131
Corcovado, 55
Costa, Lúcio, 57, 98, *109
Costa Rica, 117
Cotton industry, 71, 72, *map* 73
"Counselors," 128-129
Coups. *See* Revolts
Cruzeiro, O, magazine, 117
Cuba, 75, 133; rally for, *143
Cuiabá, 115
Culture, 97, 105, 148; in colonial mining towns, 31; imperial period, 42-43; mingling of various influences in, 84, 105; primitive Indian, 30. *See also* Architecture; Art; Folk art; Literature
Cumbica, 133
Cunha, Euclides da, 104
Currency, 26

Dairy farming, 70
Dakar, 131
Dance, 87, 88, 92
Death rate, 11
Debret, Jean-Baptiste, 101
De Lamonica, Roberto, 101
Democracy, 13, 127, 129, 135
Denys, Odilio, *138-139
Deodoro da Fonseca, Manuel, 46, 128
D'Eu, Count, 46
Diamantina, 31, 117
Diamonds, 29, 30, 31, *map* 73
Diary of Helena Morley, 117
Dictatorship, Vargas', 57, 127, 130-131
Diseases, 28, 128-129
Divorce, absence of, 11, 13, 117
Dom Casmurro, Machado de Assis, 104
Drama, folk, 87, *92-93
Drummond de Andrade, Carlos, 103
Dunham, Katherine, 113
Dutch colonization attempts, 29, 30, 72
Dutch East Indies, 74
Dutra, Eurico Gaspar, 131
Dyewood, 25, 26, 29

Economy, 69-75, 132; colonial, 30; drain of Brasília on, 57-58, 146, 148; of early Republic, 128, 129; effect of abolition of slavery on, 46, 72; Empire,

45, 46; history of, 70; inflation, 132, 145, 148; major products of, *map* 73; need of, for foreign aid, 147-148; reasons for underdevelopment of, 147-148. *See also* Agriculture; Exports; Industry; Resources

Education, 118, *120-121; of Empire period, 46; equality in, 114; need for, to overcome underdevelopment, 148; Quadros' aims in, 132; for women, 116. *See also* Illiteracy

Elections: of 1930, 129; of 1934, 130; of 1945, 131; of 1950, 131; of 1955, 131-132; of 1960, 132

Electorate, 119, 135, 145, *150-151

Electricity, 132

Emancipation of slaves, 45-46

Empire of Brazil, 42, 43-46, 130

Entertainment: of poor, 56, 83, 86, 88, 92; of rich, *19, *49-51; soccer, 12, 56, 117, *124-125. *See also* Holidays

Epitaph of a Small Winner, Machado de Assis, 104

Espírito Santo, 75

Exile's Song, Gonçalves Dias, 103

Exports: coffee, 71, 76; cotton and wool, 71; diversification of, 72; fruit and wine, 75; iron ore, 132

Extramarital relations, 11, 13

Extremists, political, 147

Family: home life, 14; ties, 10-11, 13

Farming. *See* Agriculture

Fascism, 147

Faulkner, William, 102

Favelas, 9, 11, 56, 99, *140-141, 146

Festivals. *See* Holidays

Fishing industry, 71, *map* 73

Folk art, 83-87, 92, 148; backlands poetry, 86, 87; dance, 87, 88; drama, 87, *92-93; handicrafts, 83-86; music, 85, 86-88, 101; popular sculpture, 84, 86

Fonseca e Silva, Valentim da, 100

Food: ignorance about, 11; of Indians, 37; industries, 70, 71, *map* 73, 75; lack of, 11, 28; staple diet, 15, 71, 75; transportation of, 11, 71

Ford, Henry, 74

Forests, 29, 32, *34-36, 74; exploitation of, *map* 73, 74

France, 75

French colonization attempts, 29, 30, 55

French Guiana, 71

Fruit, 29, 75

Futebol. See Soccer

Gagarin, Yuri, 86

Garden landscaping, 98-99, 109

Gauchos, 70, *map* 73

German immigrants, 84, 115

Germany (West), 133

Getúlismo, 131

Globo, 0, 148

Goiás, 30, 57, 70, 85

Gold, 28, 29, 70; discoveries of, 30, *map* 73

Golpe. See Revolts

Gomes, Eduardo, 131

Gomez, Carlos, 102, 103

Gonçalves Dias, Antônio, 103

Gonzaga, Tomás Antônio, 103

Good Hope, Cape of, 29

Goulart, João, 133, *136-137, 138, 145-146

Government: attitudes toward, 127-128; corruption in, 132; "Counselors" system of, 129; crisis (1961), 133, 137; need for improvement in, 148; under Pedro II, 44; post-Vargas, 132; present system of, 133, 137, 145-146; under Vargas, 130-131

Graham, Maria, 117

Great Britain, 42, 46

Guanabara, Bay of, 55

Guanabara, state, 72, 133

Guarany, Il, Gomez, 102

Guarnieri, Camargo, 102

Gudin, Eugenio, 148

Guevara, Ernesto, 133

Guia Prático, Villa-Lobos, 102

Handicrafts, 83-86

Haring, C. H., 42, 46

Health, 10, 28; clinics, 10, 11, *149; disease campaigns, 128-129; infant mortality, 10, 11; life expectancy, 11; malnutrition, 11

Heating, lack of, 14

Hinterlands. *See* Interior Brazil

History: arrival of Portuguese, 25-28; colonial, 29-31, 53-54; Empire, 42, 43-46; paradoxes of, 11-12; rebellion against Portugal, 31, 41, 43; Republic, 46, 128-130, 131-133; Vargas' dictatorship, 130-131

Holidays, 54; Carnival, *82-83, 87-88, *89-91; rural, 86, 87, *92-93

Horses, 70

Hospitals, 10, 11, *149

Housing, 56, 98, 99, 146; in Brasília, 58, *62-63, 146. *See also* Slums

Hugo, Victor, 44

Humor, 15

Hydroelectric power, 69, 132

Iguassú River, *35

Illegitimate birth, 13

Illiteracy, 10, 46, 118, 129; campain against, 132

Immigrants, 84, 114-115, 147

Immigration, 46, 72

Income, national, 69, 72

Inconfidência Mineira, 31, 103

Independence: achieved, 43; strife for, 31, 41

India, 70, 71

Indian Protection Service, 38, 115

Indians: at arrival of Portuguese, 26-27, 29-30, 54, 70; conversion of, 30; decimated by illnesses, 30, 37, 116; handling of problem of, 38, 115, 146; influences of, in folk art and music, 84, 85, 101, 102; surviving aborigines, 12, *36-38, 115-116

Industrialization, 72, 131, 132

Industry, 69, 72, 75, 78-79, 81; in colonial times, 30; of Empire, 42

Infant mortality, 10, 11

Inflation, 132, 145, 148

Integralistas, 130, 147

Integration, racial, 113-114, 146

Intellectuals, 15

Interior Brazil, 29, 32; colonization of, 70; "hollow frontier" of, 146; move of government to, 56-57; people of, 12, 86

Ipiranga, 43

Iron: exports, 132; industry, 42, 75; resources, 29, *map* 73, 75, *78-79

Isabel, Princess, 44, 46, 113

Israel, 117

Italian immigrants, 72, 75, 84, 115

Italy, 131

James, Henry, 103

Jangada, 71

Japanese immigrants, 84, 101, 115

Jefferson, Thomas, 31

Jesuits, 30, 100, 101

Jewelry, 85

Jews, 114

João VI, King of Portugal and Brazil, 42, 43, 101, 128

Julião, Francisco, *142

Kimberley Lode, 31

Kubitschek, Juscelino, 57, 131-132, *138, 148

Labor: agricultural, 69, 74, 142, 146; city, rise of, 129; laws, Vargas', 130; slaves, 29-30, 46, 72; strikes, 145; unions, 130

Labor party, 133

Lacemaking, 85

Lacerda, Carlos, 131, 133, *139

Lampião, bandit, 85

Land reform: demand for, 142; Quadros' plans for, 132

Landowners: under Empire, 44, 45; in Republican movement, 46, 128; today, 47

Landowski, Paul, 55

Landscaping, 98-99, 109

Language, 12; Portuguese *vs.* Spanish, 13

"Leather civilization," 70

Leather work, 84

Le Corbusier, 98

Leisure. *See* Entertainment; Holidays; Sports

Levantines, 115

Lévi-Strauss, Claude, 29

Liberalism, 44

Life expectancy, 11

Lima, Jorge de, 103

Lins do Rêgo, José, 104

Lisbôa, Antônio Francisco. *See* Aleijadinho

Lisbon, 42, 43, 99

Lispector, Clarice, 117

Literature: Minas "Arcadian" School, 31, 100, 103; poetry, 102-103; prose, 103-104; "regional" novel, 104; women writers, 117

Londrina, 72

Longfellow, Henry Wadsworth, 44

Lott, Henrique, 132

Loyola, Ignatius. *See* St. Ignatius

Luiz Pereira de Souza, Washington, 129

Lumber, *map* 73, 74

Mabe, Manabu, 101, *106

Macaws, 26

Machado de Assis, Joaquim Maria, 103-104, 114

Machine industry, 72

Maciel, Antônio, 104, 128

Macumba, 55, 85, 89; rites, *94-95

Madeira River, 115

Magalhães, Aloisio, 101

Magazines, 102

Malaya, 74

Manaus, *33, 35, 59, 69, 74, 102

Manuel I, King of Portugal, 26

Marajó, island, 71

Maranhão, 74

Maria I, Queen of Portugal, 42, 43

Maria (da Glória) II, Queen of Portugal, 43-44

Marriage, 11, 14, 116, 117; extramarital love, 11, 13; interracial, 10, 28, 84

Marvelous Journey, Putnam, 31

Matarazzo, Francisco, *81, 101

Mato Grosso, 16, 30, 115, 116; Indians of, *36, *149; products of, 70-71, 72

Mauá, Viscount, 45

Maurício, Father José, 101

Maximilian, Emperor of Mexico, 42

Meat industry, 70, 71

Meireles, Cecília, 103, 117

Mello Franco de Andrade, Rodrigo, 101

Memórias póstumas de Braz Cubas, Machado de Assis, 104

Mexico, 42

Middle class, 114, 118, 147

Mignone, Francisco, 102

Miguel, Prince, 44

Military, the, and political power, 127, 128, 129, 147. *See also* Army

Minas Conspiracy, 31, 103

Minas Gerais, 12, 32, 131; art and culture of mining towns of, 31, 85, 97, 100; colonization of, 30; economy of, 70, 71, 72, 75; political importance of, 129

"Minas Triangle," 70
Mineral resources, 29, 30, *map 73, 75, 78-79*
Mining, 75, 76, 79
Minority groups, 114-116
Miscegenation, 10, 28, 84
Missionaries, 28, 30, 100
Mississippi River, 29, 30
Mohammedans, 54, 84
Monarchism, 42, 128; pretenders, 41, 47
Moraes Barros, Prudente José de, 128
Morais, Vinícius de, 103
Moreira, Jorge M., 98
Morley, Helena, 117
Morro do Castelo, 55
Mulattoes, 54, 113, 114
Music, 101-102; folk, 83, 85, 86-88, 92

Napoleon Bonaparte, 42, 43
Natal, 130
National Liberation, Alliance of, 130
National Library, 42
Nationalism, extreme, 147
Negroes: of Bahia, 54-55; cultural influences of, 84, 85, 86, 89, 101; as slaves, 29, 30, 54 (*see also* Slavery); standing of, 113-114, 146
Neves, Tancredo, 133
"New State," Vargas', 131
Newspapers, 102, 119
Niagara Falls, 40, 44
Niemeyer, Oscar, 57, 63, 98, *108
Nuts, 29, *map* 73, 74, 75

Oil resources, 29, *map* 73, 75
Olinda, 29, 100
Order of Christ, 26
Ostrower, Fayaga, 101
Ouro Prêto, 31, 59, 100

Painting, 101, *106-107, *110
Palm trees, 74
Pantanal, 70
Paper industry, 72
Pará, 71, 84, 116
Paraguay, 45
Paraguay River, 29
Paraíba, 74
Paraná, state, 72, 74, 76, 115
Paraná River, 57, 75
Parliamentarismo, 145-146
Parties, political, 135, 147
Pascoal, Monte, 26
Paulo Afonso, falls of, 29
Peasant League, 142
Pedregulho, 98
Pedro I, Emperor, 42, 43-44, 46, 57
Pedro II, Emperor, *40, 44, *45, 46, 102, 113, 115
Peixoto, Floriano, 46, 128
People: characterization of, 10, 11, 12-15, 28, 146, 148; racial mingling of, 10, 28, 84, 113-114, 146; variety of, 12

Pernambuco, 71, 72, 74, 142
Petrobrás, 75
Petrópolis, 45, 50
Piauí, 74
Plantation system, 29, 45, 46, 47
Poetry, 102-103; Arcadian, 31, 100, 103; folk, 86, 87; romantic, 103
Polish immigrants, 84
Population, 11
Portinari, Cândido, 101, 104, *106
Pôrto Alegre, 12, 97
Pôrto Velho, 115
Portugal: as colonial power, 26-28, 29, 43, 54, 70; immigrants from, 72, 114-115; rebellion against, 31, 41, 43
Portuguese influences: in architecture, 99-100; in folk art, 84, 85, 87; in music, 101, 102
Positivist movement, 46, 128
Post, Frans, 101
Pottery, 84
Poverty, 11, 56, 114, 132, 140, 146; revolutionary forces bred by, 74, *142-143, 147
Precipitation, 28
Presidency, 127-128, 129; "coffee and milk" arrangement, 129; under new parliamentary system, 133. *See also* Government
Press, 119; under Vargas, 130, 131
Prestes, Luiz Carlos, 129, 130
Pretenders to throne, 41, 47
Prime minister, office of, 133
Protestants, 30
Public Health Service, 116
Putnam, Samuel, 31

Quadros, Anna Letycia, 101
Quadros, Jânio, 58, 86, 117, 128, 132-133, *134-135, 145, 147; letter of resignation of, 133
Queiroz, Rachel de, 104, 117
Quincas Borba, Machado de Assis, 104

Race relations, 113-114, 146. *See also* Miscegenation
Railroads, 29, 45, 75
Ramos, Graciliano, 104
Rebellion in the Backlands, da Cunha, 104
Rebouças, André, 113
Recife, 11, 86, 97, 100, 101, 146; pro-Castro rally in, *143
Refrigeration, lack of, 11, 71
Regionalism, 12, 129, 130
Reidy, Affonso Eduardo, 98
Religion, 10, 44, 123. *See also* Christianization; *Macumba*; Roman Catholic Church
Republic of Brazil, 46, 128-130, 131-133
Republican movement, 46, 128
Resources, 11, 28, *map* 73; forest, 29, 74; hydroelectric, 69, 132; mineral, 29, 30, 75
Revolts: absence of major, 15, 41; Communist (1935), 130; *golpe preventivo* (1956), 132; *Integra-*

lista (1938), 130; Minas Conspiracy, 31; of 1889, 46, 128; of 1922 and 1924, 129; of 1930, 129-130; ousters of Vargas, 131; religious, 128; of São Paulo (1932), 130
Rio de Janeiro, city: as capital, 42-43, 53, 54, 55; Carnival in, *82-83, 87, 88, *89-91; Communist revolt in (1935), 130; contemporary architecture in, *17, 98, 99; founding of, 30, 55; historical mentions of, 25, 31, 45, 100, 129-130; history of, 55; mentioned, 9, 11, 48, 50, 79, 103, 109, 117, 120, 123, 124, 133, 148, 149; modernization of, 128; municipal problems of, 146; population of, 56, 146; present-day, *16-19, *22-23, 54, 55-56, 58, *144; slums of, 9, 11, 56, *140-141, 146
Rio de Janeiro, state, 71-72
Rio Grande do Sul, 71, 75, 115, 129, 131, 133
Rio Negro, *33, *68, 74
Rivers, 29, *34-35, 69, 71, 115
Roads, 11, *24, 29, 75, 132, 146
Roman Catholic Church, 30, 44, 123; and African cults, 55; missionaries of, 28, 30, 100
Rondon, Cândido Mariano da Silva, 115
Rondônia, 115
Roosevelt, Theodore, 115
Rubber, 74

Sá, Estácio de, 55
Sailing Alone Around the World, Slocum, 14-15
St. George, 85
St. Ignatius Loyola, 28
Saint makers, 86
St. Thomas Aquinas, 102
Salvador. *See* Bahia
Samba schools, 88, 90
Santa Catarina, 74, 75, 115
Santa Cruz, 26
Santarém, 28, 116
Santos, 25, 29, 124
São Francisco, river, 29, 57, 86
São Paulo, city, 16, *19, 29, 54, *80, 81, *119; art *Bienal* in, 101, *110-111; emancipation of slaves in, 46; growth of, 72; mentioned, 14, 25, 70, 106, 113, 133
São Paulo, state, 12, 30, 71, 115; economy of, 72, 75, 76; political importance of, 129; Quadros' governorship record in, 132; rebellions in (1924, 1932), 129, 130
São Salvador da Bahia, 53. *See also* Bahia
São Sebastião do Rio de Janeiro, 30. *See also* Rio de Janeiro
São Vicente, 29
Schools, 118, *120-121
Sculpture, *96, 100; in Brasília,

*64-65; park, 25, 55; popular, 84, 86
Segall, Lasar, 101
Sertão, 74, 86. *See also* Interior Brazil
Sertões, Os, da Cunha, 104
Servants, 12-13
S.E.S.P., 116
Shipping, 29
Silva Xavier, Joaquim José da. *See* Tiradentes
Slave, The, Gomez, 103
Slave Ship, The, de Castro Alves, 103
Slavery, 14, 29-30, 45, 54; abolition of, 46, 72, 128; holdover customs, 12-13
Slocum, Joshua, 14-15
Slums, 56, *140-141, 146. *See also Favelas*
Smallpox, 129
Soccer, 12, 56, 117, *124-125
Social classes, 147; familiarity between, 12-13; middle, 114, 118; upper, 14, *47-51, 56, 104, 114, 116. *See also* Aristocracy; Labor
Social security, 130
Sousa, Irineo Evangelista de. *See* Mauá, Viscount
Sousa, Octavio Tarquinio de, 42
Southern Cross, 26; Order of, 26, 133
Souza, Thomé de, 54
Soviet Russia, 130
Spain, 26, 27, 41
S.P.H.A.N., 101
Sports: *capoeira,* 55; soccer, 12, 56, 117, *124-125
Steel industry, 69, 75, 79, 98, 131, 132
Straw weaving, 84
Strikes, 145
Students, Communist, 147
Sugar: areas, 29, 72, *map* 73, 74; importance of, in Brazilian economy, 29, 45, 54, 70, 72; labor, 74, 142
Sugar Loaf Mountain, 55, *144

Tapajós, river, 116
Taunay, Nicolas Antoine, 101
Taxes: colonial, 30; Empire, 44; evasion of, 128; reform plans, 132
Textile industry, 42, 71, 72
The '15, de Queiroz, 117
Timber, *map* 73, 74
Tiradentes (Joaquim José da Silva Xavier), 31
Tobacco industry, *map* 73, 75
Tordesillas, Treaty of, 26; dividing line of, *map* 27
Trade: Chinese-Brazilian, 133; colonial, 29, 30; foreign, 71, 72, 74, 75, 76, 132
Trade Unions, 130
Transportation, 29, 45, 69, 75, 132; of food, 11, 71
Tribuna da Imprensa, 131, 139
Tristes Tropiques, Lévi-Strauss, 29
Tupi Indians, 26

Unions, 130
United Nations, 106
United States: cattle industry of, compared with Brazil, 70, 71; cultural comparisons with Brazil, 98, 102; economic aid by, 75, 131; government system of, compared with Brazil, 133; Pedro II's visit to, *40, 44, *45, 115; relations with, 147; social comparisons with, 14, 114, 117; and Vargas regime, 130-131. *See also* American Revolution
University City, Rio, 98
Upper classes, 14, *47-51, 56, 104, 114; women of, 116
Uruguay, 45
Uruguay River, 29

Valentim, Mestre. *See* Fonseca e Silva
Valéry, Paul, 102
Vargas, Getúlio, 57, 86, *126, 129, 135; dictatorship of, 127, 130-131; political followers of, long powerful, 132, 133, 138, 145; suicide note of, 132, 133
Varnhagen, Francisco Adolfo de, 57
Vaz, Rubens Florentino, 131
Vegetation, 29, 74

Venezuela, 99
Ventre Livre, Law of, 46
Vera Cruz, Terra da, 26
Vespucci, Amerigo, 53
Vila Rica (*now* Ouro Prêto), 31
Villa-Lobos, Heitor, 102, *105
Villas Boas, Orlando, *38-39, 115
Villegaignon, Nicolas Durand de, 55
Violence, absence of, 15, 146-147
Volta Redonda, 75, 131
Voting rights, 117, 130

Washington, George, 42
Water buffalo, 71
Water shortage, 146, 147

Wealth, 11, 47, 132
Whaling, 71
Whittier, John Greenleaf, 44
Wine industry, 75
Women, 116-117; career, 117; voting right of, 117, 130
Wood carving, 86
Wool exports, 71
Work, attitudes toward, 14, 146
World War I, 129
World War II, 74, 130
Writers, 102-104; women, 117

Yellow fever, 128

Zebus, 70, 71

Production staff for Time Incorporated

Arthur R. Murphy (Vice President and Director of Production)

Robert E. Foy, James P. Menton and Caroline Ferri

Text photocomposed on Photon equipment

under the direction of Albert J. Dunn and Arthur J. Dunn

•

Printed by R. R. Donnelley & Sons Company, Crawfordsville, Indiana,

and The Safran Printing Company, Detroit, Michigan

Bound by R. R. Donnelley & Sons Company, Crawfordsville, Indiana

Paper by The Mead Corporation, Dayton, Ohio